A Well-Watered Garden
Hand-Picked Recipes From Kitchens Around the World

BCF Creative Media Product

A Well-Watered Garden

Cover Art painted by Julie Ruth
Illustrations drawn by Cheryl Miller

Printed by Carlisle Printing, 2673 TR 421, Sugarcreek, OH 44681

A Well-Watered Garden
Berlin Christian Fellowship
PO Box 396
Berlin, OH 44610

A Gift For:

"Kindness in words creates confidence.
Kindness in thinking creates profoundness.
Kindness in giving creates love." -Lao-tzu

This book is dedicated to:

All the women and children living in poverty-stricken countries and oppressed lands. May God speed the day when your gardens are blooming and prospering.

Acknowledgments:

We would like to thank all the talented people who gave of their time and expertise to make this project a success. We are blessed by your willingness to join with us.

Thanks to all those who persevered with us by typing in recipes: Ida Byer, Cindy Miller, Angie Peck, Liz Spires, Ruth Weaver, Erma Yoder

Thank you to the proofreaders for their diligence and time: Beth Ernst and Heidi Hershberger

Thank you to Bernadine Frailly for her willingness to share her wonderful poem with us.

We are so grateful to our artists, Julie Ruth (cover art) and Cheryl Miller (section pages and illustrations), for sharing your talents with us.

A special thank you to our graphic designer, Jason Torrence, for materializing our ideas and dreams into the finished project.

Finally, we want to thank all of the people who shared their ideas and advice with us throughout the making of this book. Your input was crucial to our success.

Dear Friends,

The burden of our heart is to help oppressed women and children who live in countries that are struggling against the grip of poverty. In some cases these women, who have lost their husbands in war, are faced with the impossible responsibility of providing food and clothing for their families because laws prohibit them from working. A life of struggling to survive on the streets is the result for most of these families. In other cases, these families are slowly dying from malnutrition and starvation in famine-stricken countries with no hope for the future. Our hearts are breaking for these people as we learn more about their lives. We want to do something to make a difference. Our mission is to reach out to these families and help provide relief for them in whatever way we can. We are dedicated to this goal. We will no longer sit by and watch!

We are looking for springs of life to break forth in the dry, parched lands of the world. The Word of God promises us springs that will never run dry and life as a WELL-WATERED GARDEN!

We believe that when we feed those who are hungry and take care of the needs of those who are in trouble, then our light will shine in the darkness and we will be bright like sunshine at noon. And the Lord will always lead us; He will satisfy our needs in dry lands and give strength to our bones. We will be like a well-watered garden, like a spring that never runs dry. Those from among us shall build the old waste places. We shall raise up the foundations of many generations, and we will be called the Repairer of the Breach, the Restorers of Streets to Dwell In. (Isaiah 58:10-12)

Our mission is two-fold: to create revenue to assist women and children who live in oppressed, poverty-stricken nations by providing food, clothing and necessary supplies; and to provide an avenue for people to share their favorite recipes and broaden our palettes through international dishes. Within the pages of this cookbook, you will find a variety of recipes, from hometown to elegant, from international basics to exotic delights. These recipes have been gathered from the cooks at Berlin Christian Fellowship in Berlin, Ohio, and from our friends all over the globe. It is our desire to offer you something different, something tasty, something beyond the norm. We hope you thoroughly enjoy the recipes found within A WELL-WATERED GARDEN.

Dedicated to serving others,

Erma Yoder   Heidi Hershberger
Angie Peck   Mandy Beachy

Father Feed the Children

Fruit and nuts and berries
Growing ripe and sweet
Vegetables and golden corn
All for us to eat.

Rich food in its plenty
Picked and stored away
While others in their countries
Are starving every day.

Mothers in the market
Choosing what to eat.
Perhaps a rich fruit pudding
For a special treat.

In heats of Ethiopia
Little grows on land
A mother looks at the food for the day
Which only feeds one hand.

In lands of drought and hunger
"No more—Dear Lord" we pray
Will mothers ask the question:

Which child to feed today?

-Bernadine Frailly

Table of Contents

Normal day, let me be aware of the treasure you are.

Let me learn from you, love you, bless you before you depart.

Let me not pass you by in quest of some rare and perfect tomorrow.

-Mary Jean Iron

Beverages, Snacks, & Appetizers

Christmas Punch

13 c. water
4 c. sugar
92 oz. pineapple juice,
  unsweetened

12 oz. lemon juice
1 oz. almond extract
Gingerale
1 small package of
  red jello

In a large pot, heat water and dissolve jello and sugar. Add lemon juice, almond extract and pineapple juice. Freeze in 1 qt. containers. Remove from freezer about 2 hours before serving. Add a 2 qt. bottle of gingerale to each 1 qt. of punch concentrate. Freeze some punch in a ring mold for an ice ring. This punch is best when slushy. Makes approximately 6 qt. of concentrate plus 2 ice rings.

-Cheryl Miller

Party Punch

1 pkg. cherry Kool-Aid
1 pkg. strawberry Kool-Aid
6 oz. frozen concentrated
  orange juice
6 oz. frozen concentrated
  lemonade

1 1/2 c. sugar
3 qt. water
2 c. gingerale or 7-UP

Mix Kool-Aids, orange juice, lemonade, sugar, and water together. Add gingerale just before serving. Serves 10-12 people.

-Alma Spires

Cranberry Punch

1 large bottle cranberry cocktail
2 large bottles gingerale
48 oz. pineapple juice

1 c. sugar
1/4 c. Realemon
1 c. grapefruit juice

Mix ingredients together well and add ice. Serves 10-12 people.

-Kathy Marner

"Cheerfully share your home with those
who need a meal or a place to stay."
1 Peter 4:9

Cranberry Punch

64 oz. cranberry juice
48 oz. pineapple juice
1/4 c. lemon juice

1 bottle gingerale
1/2-1 c. sugar
1 c. grapefruit juice

*Mix ingredients together well and add ice. This fills
a punch bowl.*

-Naomi Gingerich

Tea

Tea of your choice:
  Earl Grey, Constant Comment,
  English Breakfast, Mint or
  Lemon

Water
Optional: sugar,
  lemon & cream

Fill teapot with water, bringing it to a boil. Empty teapot and put tea leaves (in strainer) 1 tsp. per cup. Water must be boiling when poured over tea leaves. Steep tea for 3-5 minutes. Pour and enjoy. NOTE: Tea must be made in a china pot.

-Kathy Torrence

Gretchen's Iced Tea

1 c. sugar
2 c. water
2 pinches baking soda

8 Lipton tea bags
2 c. crushed ice
lemon (optional)

Bring water to a boil. Remove from heat; add sugar, baking soda and tea bags. Steep 20 minutes. Remove tea bags and add ice. Serve with lemon. Serves 4 people.

-Charlene Miller

Two Fruit Frosty

1 1/2 c. red raspberries,
fresh or frozen
1 c. frozen unsweetened,
sliced peaches (thawed)
1 c. milk

8 oz. vanilla yogurt
1/3 c. honey
1/2 tsp. cinnamon
1/2 tsp. nutmeg
Cinnamon stick
(optional)

Combine raspberries, peaches and milk in a blender. Cover and process on high. Add yogurt, honey, cinnamon and nutmeg. Blend well then pour into glasses. Garnish with a cinnamon stick. Serve immediately. Serves 4 people.

-Katie Barkman

Mocha Punch

1 1/2 qt. water
1/2 c. instant chocolate
milk drink mix
1/4 c. instant coffee granules
1 c. whipped cream
chocolate curls (optional)

1/2 gal. vanilla ice
cream
1/2 c. white sugar
1/2 gal. chocolate
ice cream

In a large saucepan bring water to boil. Remove from heat. Add drink mix, sugar and coffee. Stir until dissolved. Cover and refrigerate for 4 hours or overnight. Approximately 30 minutes before serving, pour into punch bowl. Add ice cream by scoopful. Stir until partially melted. Garnish with dollops of whipped cream and chocolate curls. Yield: approximately 5 qts. Serves 20-25 people.

-Katie Barkman

Christmas Tea

2 c. instant tea mix
1/2-1 c. red hot candies
1 pkg. lemonade Kool-Aid mix

2 c. Tang
1 c. sugar
1/2 tsp. ground
cloves

To prepare tea mixture combine ingredients together and store in an airtight container. To prepare tea, mix 1 tsp. of tea mixture with 1 c. boiling water.

-Katie Barkman

Hot Cranberry Punch

8 c. water, hot
1 1/2 c. sugar
3/4 c. orange juice
12 whole cloves (optional)

1/4 c. lemon juice
4 c. cranberry juice
1/2 c. red hot candies

In a 5 qt. crockpot, combine water, sugar and juices. Stir until sugar is dissolved. Place cloves in a cheesecloth and tie together. Place cloves and candies in the crockpot. Cover and cook on low for 2-3 hours until heated through. Discard cheesecloth before serving. Yield: 3 1/2 qt.

-Carol S. Miller

6

Nepali Chai

"A kind word is like a spring day."
Russian Proverb

1/2 c. water
1 tsp. Taj Mahal Tea
1/4 tsp. Kamal Tea Masale
  or 1 pinch of each: cordamom,
  ginger, cloves and cinnamon

1/2 c. whole milk
2 tsp. sugar

Combine ingredients together in a pan and almost bring to a boiling point. Let sit for a couple of minutes. Run it through a strainer and enjoy. NOTE: This is a drink our family enjoys.

-Erma Yoder

Hot Chocolate Mix

10 c. dry milk
11 oz. non-dairy creamer

1 lb. Nestles Quik
1 c. powdered sugar

Mix ingredients together well. To prepare stir 1/3 c. mix to 1 c. of hot water. Store remaining mix in a covered container.

-Dean & Arvilla Kaufman

Cappuccino Mix

1 c. instant coffee creamer
2/3 c. instant coffee crystals
1 1/2 tsp. ground cinnamon

1 c. Nestles Quik
1/3 c. sugar
1 tsp. ground nutmeg

To prepare cappuccino mixture combine all ingredients and mix well. Store in an airtight container. To prepare cappuccino add 3 heaping tsp. to 1 c. hot water; stir well. Place some whipped topping and a pinch of nutmeg on top. Fill pint jars with dry mix and give away as gifts. Yield: 3 c. dry mix.

-Erma Yoder

Cheese Ball

16 oz. cream cheese,
  softened
1/2 lb. cheddar cheese,
  shredded
1 Tbsp. onion, chopped fine
1 Tbsp. Worcestershire sauce

1 Tbsp. parsley
1 Tbsp. Realemon
1 1/2 c. walnuts,
  chopped

Mix ingredients together and roll in chopped walnuts. Refrigerate until ready to serve. Serves 8-10 people.

-Kathy Marner

Cheese Ball

16 oz. cream cheese
1 lb. Velveeta cheese,
  shredded
2 Tbsp. Worcestershire sauce
Small onion, chopped

2 Tbsp. Realemon
1 green pepper,
  chopped
1/2 box Ritz crackers
1 1/2 c. walnuts,
  chopped

With hands, mix ingredients together except nuts and crackers. Form into a ball. Roll in walnuts. Place on a plate and surround with Ritz crackers.

-Louise Marner

Garden Party Cheese Ball

16 oz. cream cheese,
  softened
1/4 c. onions, chopped
1/2 c. Real Bacon Bits
1 tsp. seasoned salt
Pinch of salt

1 c. cheddar cheese,
  shredded
1 c. mozzarella cheese
1 celery, chopped
1 c. walnuts, chopped

Mix ingredients together except walnuts. Form into a ball and roll in walnuts, coating the outside of ball. Place on a serving plate and serve with crackers. NOTE: You can add about 1 or 2 Tbsp. of milk if you like a softer cheese ball.

-Katie Barkman

9

Cheese Ball

8 oz. cream cheese
1/2 c. crushed pineapple, drained
1/2 c. green peppers, chopped

1 c. crushed nuts
1 Tbsp. onion
1 tsp. seasoned salt

Mix ingredients together except for 1/2 c. nuts. Form into a ball and place on a festive plate. Cover with remaining nuts and serve with crackers.

-Naomi Gingerich

Easy Cheesy Dip

16 oz. refried beans
2 c. cheddar cheese, shredded

1 pkg. taco seasoning
1 pt. sour cream

Mix refried beans and taco seasoning together. Spread in 13"x9" baking pan. Spread sour cream on top of bean mixture. Sprinkle cheese on top. Bake at 350° for 30 minutes. Serve with corn chips while hot from the oven.

-Lynette Miller

Mexican Dip

1 can bean dip
1 small onion, chopped
1 large tomato, chopped
1/2 c. salsa
1 pkg. taco seasoning
1-2 c. cheddar cheese, grated

2 large avocados
1 tsp. lemon juice
Dash of garlic salt
8 oz. sour cream
1/2 c. mayonnaise

Use a serving dish approximately 8"x8 ". Spread bean dip across bottom of the dish. Blend avocados in food processor. Add lemon juice, garlic salt, onions, salsa, and half of the tomatoes. Spread over bean dip. Mix sour cream, mayonnaise and taco seasoning. Spread over avacado mixture. Place cheese and remaining tomatoes on top. Serve with corn chips.

-Heidi Smith

Creamy Salsa Dip

1 c. Hellman's mayonnaise
1 pkg. Knorr vegetable
  soup mix

1 c. sour cream
12 oz. salsa

Mix ingredients together. Chill for 2 hours. Serve with tortilla chips.

-Carol Miller

Fresh Peach Salsa

2 c. fresh peaches, chopped
1/4 c. sweet onions, chopped
2-3 Tbsp. seeded jalapeno pepper, finely chopped

3 Tbsp. lime juice
1 clove garlic, minced
1 Tbsp. fresh cilantro, snipped
1/2 tsp. sugar

In a medium mixing bowl, stir ingredients together. Cover and chill 1-2 hours. Serve this spunky salsa with tortilla chips, pork, chicken, fish or Mexican dishes. Yield: 2 cups.

-Mabel Campbell

Baked Onion Dip

1 c. sweet onion, chopped
1 Tbsp. Parmesan cheese
1 c. Swiss cheese, shredded
Minced parsley (optional)

1 c. mayonnaise
1/4 tsp. garlic salt

In a bowl combine mayonnaise, onion, cheeses, parsley and garlic salt. Place in 1 qt. baking dish. Bake uncovered at 350° for 40 minutes. Yield: 2 cups.

-Carol S. Miller

Hot Taco Cheese Dip

2 lb. Velveeta cheese, cubed
2 cans cream of mushroom
  soup
1 can nacho cheese soup
1 bottle mild taco sauce
1 green pepper, chopped

1 lb. hamburger
Garlic salt (to taste)
Chili powder (to taste)
1/4 tsp. red pepper

Fry hamburger; drain grease. Add soups, cheese, taco sauce and peppers. Simmer on low until cheese is melted. Add garlic salt and chili powder. Transfer to a crockpot. Keep warm on low for a gathering or party. Serve with corn chips or tortilla chips.

-Sharon Gerber

Crab Dip

1 lb. crabmeat
1 tsp. Worcestershire sauce
8 oz. cream cheese
1 tsp. liquid crab boil

1 stick butter
Salt (to taste)
Red pepper (to taste)

Melt butter and cream cheese then add crabmeat. Season with liquid crab boil, salt, red pepper, and Worcestershire sauce. Serves 20-25 people.

-Jeannette Grant
(First Baptist Church, Dover, OH)

Hot Crab Dip

24 oz. cream cheese,
  cubed
16 oz. imitation crabmeat,
  flaked
4 oz. green chilies, chopped

1/2 c. milk
1/3 c. salsa
1 c. green onions,
  thinly sliced

Combine milk and salsa. Transfer to a crockpot, coated with nonstick cooking spray. Stir in cream cheese, crabmeat, onions and chilies. Cover and cook on low for 3-4 hours, stirring every 30 minutes. Serve with crackers. Yield: approximately 5 c.

-Ann Miller

Microwaveable Caramel Corn

1 c. brown sugar
1 stick butter or oleo
1/4 tsp. salt
2 c. nuts (optional)

1/4 tsp. baking soda
1/4 c. corn syrup
3-4 qt. popped corn

In a 2 qt. microwave-safe dish, melt butter then add brown sugar, salt and corn syrup. Boil for 2 minutes. Remove from microwave and stir in baking soda. Put popped corn in a grocery bag. Pour syrup mixture over corn. Close bag and shake. Microwave in bag 1 1/2 minutes. Stir then cook another 1 1/2 minutes. Open, stir and eat. NOTE: The corn gets covered better if you stir the corn rather than shaking it. For variation add 2 c. nuts.

-Jim Weiss

Caramel Corn

7 qt. popped corn
1/2 c. light Karo
2 sticks butter
1 tsp. vanilla

2 c. brown sugar
1 tsp. salt
1/2 tsp. soda

Boil brown sugar, Karo, butter and salt for 5 minutes. Remove from stove and add soda and vanilla. Pour over popcorn. Mix well. Put in cake pans and bake at 250° for 1 hour. Stir several times during baking.

-Carol Miller

Puppy Chow

6 c. Crispix cereal
1/4 c. peanut butter

6 oz. chocolate chips
1 c. powdered sugar

In a large microwave-safe bowl, melt chocolate chips on high for 1 minute. Stir and heat an additional 30 seconds on high or until melted. Stir in peanut butter. Gently stir Crispix cereal into chocolate mixture until well coated. Place powdered sugar in a 2 gallon storage bag. Add coated cereal to sugar and close bag. Gently toss cereal mixture until well coated. Store in an airtight container in refrigerator. Yield: approximately 8 cups.

-Tara Lynn Smith

Honey Glazed Crispix Mix

8 c. Crispix mix
3 c. pretzels
1/2 c. honey

2 c. pecan halves
2/3 c. butter

Combine Crispix, pretzels and pecans. Melt butter and honey; mix well. Pour over Crispix mixture until well coated. Place on 2 well greased cookie sheets. Bake at 350° for 12-15 minutes. When finished baking, cool mixture on a paper bag. Break apart. Yummy!

-Ann Miller

Nutty Cracker Delights

42 Club crackers
1/2 c. sugar
1 c. almonds, slivered

1/2 c. butter or oleo
1 tsp. vanilla

Place crackers in a single layer in a foil-lined 15"x10" baking pan. In a saucepan over medium heat, melt butter then add sugar. Bring to a boil, stirring constantly. Boil for 2 minutes; remove from heat and add vanilla. Pour evenly over crackers, sprinkle with nuts. Bake at 350° for 10-12 minutes or until lightly browned. Immediately remove from the pan, cutting between crackers if necessary. Cool on wire racks.

-Becky Yerian

Oat Snack Mix

1/2 c. butter
1/4 c. brown sugar, packed
1/2 tsp. salt
1 1/2 c. old-fashioned oats
1 c. small pretzels

1/3 c. honey
1 tsp. cinnamon
3 c. square oat cereal
1 c. mixed nuts

In a saucepan or microwave-safe bowl, combine butter, honey, brown sugar, cinnamon and salt. Heat until butter is melted. Stir until sugar is dissolved. In a large bowl combine cereal, oats, nuts and pretzels. Drizzle with butter mixture and mix well. Place in greased 5"x10" baking pan. Bake uncovered at 275° for 45 minutes. Stir every 15 minutes. Cool for 15 minutes, stirring occasionally. Store in an airtight container. Yield: approximately 6 c.

-Joanne Weaver

TV Snacks

Snack Mixture:
6 c. Kix
4 c. Cheerios
4 c. Rice Chex
6 c. pretzels
2 lb. mixed nuts, coarsely
  chopped

Sauce:
1 c. butter, melted
2 tsp. Worcestershire
  sauce
1 tsp. garlic salt
  (optional)
1 tsp. soy sauce

Combine snack mixture ingredients together in a large bowl. Combine sauce mixture ingredients and pour over snack mixture. Bake in large pans at 250° for 1 hour. Stir every 15 minutes.

-Chris Bower

Turkish Dolma
Stuffed Grapevine Leaves Cooked
in Olive Oil

12 oz. grapevine
  leaves, pickled
1 1/2 c. rice
6 c. olive oil
2 oz. pine nuts
1 lb. onion, minced
1 tsp. salt

1 tsp. sugar
1 oz. currants, dried
Parsley
Mint
Dill
1 lemon
2 1/2 c. water, hot

Wash rice in warm water and drain. Place some olive oil in a saucepan. Lightly fry pine nuts in the oil. Add onion and fry. Stir in salt, sugar and dried currants. Add water, cooking for 15 minutes. Cool. When cooled, add parsley, mint and dill. Place stuffing mixture on grapevine leaves and roll. Place stuffed dolmas side by side in a saucepan. Add olive oil, salt, sugar and water and cook for 40-45 minutes. Serve cold. You can replace grapevine leaves with eggplant, bell pepper or tomatoes.

NOTE from submitter: The Turkish word "Dolma" literally means stuffed. It is also the word they use for their public mini buses, which should give you a good idea what public transportation in Turkey is often like. This delectable appetizer is a favorite all over the Middle East, despite the work necessary to make it. You can also use potatoes for stuffing. Enjoy one of my favorite Turkish foods!

-Lewis Kaufman
(Recipe by Chef Feridün Ügümü)

18

Spinach Deviled Eggs

12 hard-boiled eggs
2 Tbsp. butter, softened
1 tsp. sugar
1/2 c. spinach, chopped,
  thawed and squeezed dry
4 bacon strips, cooked
  and crumbled

1/4 c. mayonnaise
2 Tbsp. vinegar
1/2 tsp. pepper
1/4 tsp. salt

Slice eggs in half lengthwise. Remove yolks and set whites aside. In a small bowl mash yolks with a fork. Stir in mayonnaise, vinegar, butter, sugar, pepper and salt. Add spinach and mix well. Stir in bacon. Spoon mixture into egg whites. Yield: 2 dozen

-Carol S. Miller

Salsa Strips

2 tubes crescent rolls
1 1/2 c. salsa
2 c. mozzarella cheese,
  shredded

4 Tbsp. Dijon mustard
Parsley
Cilantro

Unroll crescent roll dough and separate into 4 rectangles. Place on greased baking sheets. Spread mustard and salsa on each rectangle. Bake at 350° for 10 minutes. Sprinkle with cheese and bake for 8-10 minutes longer until golden brown. Cool. Cut into 4 strips. Sprinkle with parsley and cilantro. Serves 12 people.

-Carol S. Miller

Lite Cheese-Stuffed Mushrooms

1 lb. mushrooms, fresh
2 tsp. butter
4 Tbsp. low-fat
  cottage cheese
3 Tbsp. seasoned
  bread crumbs

1 small onion
1 Tbsp. parsley
Salt (to taste)
Pepper (to taste)
Garlic powder
  (to taste)

Preheat oven broiler. Wash mushrooms and remove stems. Simmer stems for 2 minutes in onions and butter. Add parsley, cottage cheese and bread crumbs. Mix and season with salt, pepper and garlic powder. Stuff into mushroom caps and arrange on broiler pan. Broil until lightly browned.

-Christina Troyer

"Fresh" Salsa

3-4 Roma tomatoes,
  chopped
1 small onion or 1 bunch
  of green onions, chopped
2 Tbsp. fresh garlic, chopped
1 small jar taco sauce
  (not salsa)

10 oz. tomatoes, diced
10 oz. green chilies
salt (to taste)
pepper (to taste)
1/4 c. fresh cilantro,
  chopped

Mix ingredients together and serve.

-Vicki Yoder

Salmon Tartlets

"The Kingdom of Heaven is like a net that was let down
into the lake and caught all kinds of fish."
Matthew 13:47

DOUGH:
1/2 c. butter, softened
3 oz. cream cheese,
  softened

1 c. all-purpose flour

FILLING:
2 eggs
1/2 c. milk
1 Tbsp. butter, melted
1 tsp. lemon juice
1/2 c. dry bread crumbs
14 3/4 oz. salmon, drained
  and deboned

1 1/2 tsp. dried
  parsley flakes
1/2 tsp. rubbed sage
  or rosemary
1/2 tsp. salt
1/4 tsp. pepper
1 green onion

*Combine dough ingredients in a mixing bowl. Beat until
smooth. Shape dough by the tablespoonful into balls. Press
dough into bottom and up the sides of greased miniature
muffin cups. To make filling, combine eggs, milk, butter and
lemon juice in a bowl. Stir in crumbs, parsley, sage or rosemary, salt and pepper. Fold in salmon and onion. Spoon into
dough. Bake at 350° for 30-35 minutes or until browned.
Yield:*
2 dozen

-Dean and Arvilla Kaufman

Hawaiian Chicken Wings

2 lbs. wingettes or drumettes   Flour

SAUCE:
1 c. soy sauce   1 Tbsp. sesame oil
2-3 cloves garlic, grated   2 Tbsp. sesame seed
4 green onions, chopped   1/2 c. brown sugar

Coat chicken with flour and refrigerate overnight in a paper
bag. Fry wings in 1" of oil until light brown. Cool. Combine
sauce ingredients. Dip chicken in sauce and place on a
cookie sheet. Place in warm oven until sauce is set and
chicken is reheated.

-Erma Yoder

"Prayer reaches out to a dying world
and says, 'I care.'"
1 Peter 4:9

Buffalo Chicken Wings

"Friendship is the source of the greatest pleasures, and without friends even the most agreeable pursuits become tedious." St. Thomas Aquinas

Vegetable oil
1/4 c. butter
1/4 c. Crystal Louisiana
  Hot Sauce or Franks Red
  Hot Cayenne Sauce
Dash of ground pepper
Dash of garlic powder
Blue Cheese dressing

1/2 c. all-purpose
  flour
1/4 tsp. paprika
1/4 tsp. cayenne
  pepper
1/4 tsp. salt
10 chicken wings
Celery sticks

Heat oil at 375° in a deep fryer. Use just enough to cover the wings entirely (an inch or so deep at least). Combine butter, hot sauce, ground pepper and garlic powder in a small saucepan over low heat. Heat until butter is melted and ingredients are well blended. Combine flour, paprika, cayenne pepper and salt in a small bowl. If wings are frozen, thaw and dry them. Place wings in a large bowl and sprinkle flour mixture over them, coating each wing evenly. Place wings in the refrigerator for 60-90 minutes. (This will help breading to stick to wings when fried.) Place all wings in the hot oil and fry for 10-15 minutes or until some parts of wings begin to turn dark brown. Remove wings from oil. Drain on a paper towel. Do not let them sit too long because you want to serve hot wings. Quickly put the wings in a large bowl with a lid. Add the hot sauce and stir, coating all the wings evenly. Put the lid back on, then shake. Serve with Blue Cheese dressing and celery sticks on the side.

-Marlin Yoder

Chicken Roll-ups

1 small onion,
  chopped fine
1/2 green pepper,
  finely chopped

1 large can white
  chicken meat,
  chopped
12 oz. cream cheese
8 tortillas

Mix onion, green pepper, chicken and cream cheese together. Spread on tortillas and roll up. Refrigerate overnight. Slice roll-ups into 1/4" pieces and serve.

-Angie Gerber

Hot Pepper Poppers

Hot peppers, halved and
  seeded
1/4 tsp. garlic powder
1/4 c. real bacon bits
1/4 tsp. chili powder
8 oz. cream cheese, softened

8 oz. sharp cheddar
  cheese, shredded
1/2 c. Parmesan
  cheese, grated
Italian bread crumbs

Combine garlic powder, bacon bits, chili powder and cheeses. Fill peppers with cream cheese mixture. Sprinkle with Italian bread crumbs. Bake at 300° for 30 minutes or until bubbly.

-Jess Schrock

Party Meatballs

2 lb. ground beef
1/2 c. bread crumbs
1/4 c. milk
1 egg, beaten
8 oz. grape or apple jelly

Salt (to taste)
Pepper (to taste)
14 oz. tomato
  ketchup

Mix ground beef, bread crumbs, milk, egg, salt and pepper together. Form into small balls for appetizers. Brown meatballs in a skillet. Drain and set aside. In a separate bowl, mix ketchup and jelly. Add meatballs and simmer in a covered saucepan for 20-30 minutes.

-Lynette Miller

Bacon Chestnuts

2 cans whole
  water chestnuts

1 lb. bacon

SAUCE:
1 c. ketchup

1 c. brown sugar

Wrap 1 piece of bacon around each water chestnut and secure with a toothpick. Bake at 350° for 30 minutes. Drain fat. Combine sauce ingredients together. Pour sauce over chestnuts and bake another 30 minutes. Bake them in a cake pan on a cooling rack. NOTE: This works well so the fat can drain off.

-Steve and Lori Frink

Swedish Meatballs
Aunt Cheryl's Special Recipe

MEAT:

1 1/2 lb. hamburger
1 1/2 lb. sausage
1 tsp. salt
1 small onion, chopped

Pepper
1 tsp. oregano
2 eggs
1 tsp. garlic powder

SAUCE:

15 oz. tomato sauce
1/2 tsp. oregano
1/2 tsp. parsley
1/2 tsp. salt

1/2 tsp. basil
1/2 tsp. garlic
1/4 c. brown sugar

Mix meat ingredients together and roll into balls. In a separate bowl, mix sauce ingredients together. Place raw meatballs into electric skillet and top with sauce. Simmer at least 2 hours. NOTE: The longer you cook them, the better they are.

-Dena Green

Rumaki

1 c. ketchup
1 c. brown sugar
2 Tbsp. BBQ sauce
1 tsp. Worcestershire sauce

1 tsp. soy sauce
1 lb. bacon
2 cans whole
  water chestnuts

Cut bacon in thirds. Drain water chestnuts. Wrap 1 bacon slice around each water chestnut. Secure with a toothpick. Place on a baking sheet and broil in oven until bacon is cooked. Place in a crockpot. Mix remaining ingredients and pour on top. Heat through.

-Teresea Morris

Bite Size
Taco Turnovers

10 oz. pizza dough
1/4 c. cheddar cheese,
  shredded

1 egg
1 tsp. water

FILLING:
1/2 lb. ground beef
1/4 c. taco sauce
1 1/2 tsp. chili powder

1/4 tsp. onion powder
1/4 tsp. garlic powder

To make filling, cook ground beef in a small skillet until brown. Drain fat. Stir in taco sauce, chili powder, onion powder and garlic powder. Set aside. Roll dough into a 14"x10" 1/2" rectangle. Cut into 12, 3 1/2" squares. Divide filling among dough squares. Sprinkle with cheese. Brush edges with water. Lift one corner of each square and stretch dough to opposite corner, making a triangle. Press edges well with a fork to seal. Arrange on a greased baking sheet. Prick with a fork. Combine egg and water. Brush onto turnovers. Bake at 425° for 8-10 minutes. Let stand 5 minutes before serving. Serves 12 people.

-Ruth Weaver

"Wherever there is a human being, there is an
opportunity to share kindness."
-Marcus Annaeus Seneca

"A modest garden contains, for those who
know how to look and to wait, more
instruction than a library."

-Henri Frederic Amiel

Breads, Muffins,
& Breakfast

Pumpkin Bread

5 eggs
1 1/4 c. oil
15 oz. pumpkin
2 small pkg. cook-and-serve
  vanilla pudding mix
1 tsp. ground cinnamon

2 c. all-purpose flour
2 c. sugar
1/2 tsp. salt
1 tsp. baking soda

Beat eggs in a mixing bowl. Add oil and pumpkin; beat until smooth. In a separate bowl, combine pudding, cinnamon, flour, sugar, salt and baking soda. Gradually beat into pumpkin mixture. Pour batter into 5 greased loaf pans (5"x2 1/2"). Bake at 325° for 50-55 minutes or until an inserted toothpick comes out clean. Cool for 10 minutes. Remove from pans and place on wire racks. Cool completely. Yield: 5 loaves. NOTE: Bread may also be baked in 2 greased 8"x4" loaf pans for 75-80 minutes.

-Jess Schrock

Cranberry Bread

2 c. flour
1 c. sugar
1 1/2 tsp. baking powder
1/2 tsp. baking soda
1 tsp. salt
1 egg, well beaten
2 c. cranberries, coarsely chopped

3/4 c. orange juice
1 Tbsp. grated
  orange rind
3 Tbsp. oil
1/2 c. nuts

Sift flour, sugar, baking powder, baking soda and salt together and mix well. Combine egg, orange juice, rind and oil. Add egg mixture to dry mixture. Mix together until dampened. Carefully fold in nuts and cranberries. Bake at 350° for 1 hour.

-Erma Yoder

Zucchini Bread
Orange-Flavored

2 c. zucchini, grated
3 eggs, slightly beaten
1 c. cooking oil
3 tsp. orange extract
3 c. flour
1 1/2 c. sugar
1 tsp. salt

1 tsp. baking powder
1 tsp. baking soda
1 c. walnuts or pecans,
chopped
3 Tbsp. concentrated
orange juice
Zest from 1 orange

GLAZE:
Confectioners' sugar   Orange juice

*Wash and grate zucchini, including the peeling and juice.
Combine eggs, oil and orange extract. Mix flour, sugar, salt,
baking powder and baking soda. Add to egg mixture. Add
zucchini, nuts, concentrated orange juice and zest. Grease
loaf pans and fill 1/2 full. Bake at 350° for 1 hour. After
cooled, glaze with confectioners' sugar and orange juice mixture. Serves 12 people.*

-Ida G. Byer

Southern Spoon Bread

1 c. cornmeal
2 Tbsp. butter or margarine
3 c. milk

4 eggs, beaten
1 c. milk
1/2 tsp. salt

*Combine cornmeal, butter and 3 cups of milk in a saucepan.
Bring to a boil, stirring constantly. When thickened, remove
from heat. Add eggs, 1 cup of milk and salt. Beat well. Pour
into a 2 qt. greased casserole dish. Bake for 45 minutes. Serve
with hot butter. Serves 6-8 people.*

-Alma Spires

Date Nut Loaf

1 1/2 c. flour
1 1/2 c. sugar
1 tsp. baking powder
1 tsp. salt
2 lbs. dates, pitted
8 oz. maraschino cherries,
  drained

2 lbs. walnuts, shelled
1 lb. Brazil nuts
5 large eggs
1 tsp. vanilla

Sift flour, sugar, baking powder and salt into a large mixing bowl. Add nuts and fruit to flour mixture; stir until well coated. In a separate bowl, beat eggs until mixed, then stir in vanilla. Stir egg mixture into nut mixture until everything is well coated. Grease 5 loaf pans. Fill each pan approximately 1/2 full. Bake in a slow oven at 325° for 1 hour or until browned. Cool before slicing. NOTE: Great replacement for fruitcake for the holidays.

-Andrew J. Brugger

Banana Nut Bread

2 c. flour
1/2 c. butter
1/2 tsp. baking powder
1/2 tsp. salt
1 c. bananas, mashed
1 tsp. cinnamon

1 c. sugar
2 eggs
1/2 tsp. baking soda
1/2 c. nuts, chopped
3 Tbsp. buttermilk

Mix ingredients together and pour into greased bread pan. Bake at 350° for 45 minutes - 1 hour. Serves 12 people.

-Jeannette Grant
(First Baptist Church, Dover, OH)

Irish Soda Bread

4 c. flour
1/4 c. sugar
1 tsp. salt
1 tsp. baking powder
1 tsp. baking soda
1/4 c. margarine
3 - 4 Tbsp. caraway seeds

2 c. raisins
1 1/3 c. lowfat
  buttermilk
2 egg whites, beaten
Milk

Combine flour, sugar, salt, baking powder, and baking soda. Cut in margarine until mixture resembles coarse meal. Stir in caraway seeds and raisins. In a separate bowl combine buttermilk and egg whites. Mix into dry mixture until moistened. Turn out onto floured surface and knead lightly until smooth. Shape dough into a ball and place in a 7" round loaf pan. Cut a 4" cross about 1/4" deep into the top. Brush the top with milk. Bake at 375° for 1 hour or until golden brown.

-Erma Yoder

Round Cheese Bread

1 1/2 c. biscuit baking mix
1 c. mozzarella cheese,
  shredded
1/4 c. Parmesan cheese,
  grated

1/2 tsp. oregano, dried
1/2 c. milk
1 egg, beaten
2 Tbsp. oil or butter,
  melted

Combine all ingredients together in a bowl, except butter. Spoon into an 8" round baking pan. Drizzle with butter. Sprinkle with additional Parmesan cheese. Bake for 20 - 25 minutes. Cool for 10 minutes. Cut into wedges. Serves 6-8 people.

-Carol S. Miller

Mexican-Style Corn Bread

1/2 c. butter
1/3 c. Mexican or
  whole wheat flour
1/4 c. water
1 1/2 c. corn

1/4 c. cornmeal
1/3 c. sugar
2 Tbsp. cream
1/4 tsp. salt
1/2 tsp. baking powder

*Beat ingredients together and place in a lightly greased 9"
baking dish. Place in a pan of water (like custard). Cover and
bake at 350°-375° for 45-60 minutes. Serve by the scoopful
(small cookie scoop).Yum! Almost like Chi Chi's.*

-Marilyn Hartman

Thank God for dirty dishes;
they have a tale to tell.

While other folks go hungry,
we're eating pretty well.

With home, and health, and happiness,
We shouldn't want to fuss;

For by this stack of evidence,
God's very good to us.

-Anonymous

Brown Bread

1 1/2 c. raisins, seedless
1 1/2 c. water
2 tsp. baking soda
1 c. sugar
1 egg, beaten

2 Tbsp. oil or
  shortening, melted
2 3/4 c. flour
Pinch of salt

Boil water and raisins; add soda while hot. Add remaining ingredients and stir. Pour into 3 or 4 greased tin cans (use Campbell's soup size). Fill them 1/2 - 2/3 full. Bake at 350° for 45 minutes. After baking, lay cans on their sides to cool. When cool take them out of the cans and slice. You will have nice sized pieces. Serves 4 - 5 people.

-Fern Begly

Cinnamon Raisin Bread

2 pkg. yeast
1 1/2 c. water, warm
1 1/2 c. water, boiling
1 1/2-2 c. raisins
1 c. oatmeal

1 1/2 Tbsp. cinnamon
1/2 c. Karo syrup
2 tsp. salt
2 Tbsp. butter
7-8 c. flour

Dissolve yeast in warm water. Let stand 5 minutes. Pour boiling water over raisins, butter and oatmeal. Let stand 15 minutes. Add Karo and salt. Combine flour and cinnamon. Add to cooled mixtures, 1 cup at a time. Knead until smooth. Put into greased bowl and cover with cloth. Let rise until double, approximately 1 hour-1 hour and fifteen minutes. Knead down and let rise again, 45 minutes-1 hour. Knead down, divide into 3 parts and put into 3 greased bread pans. Let rise until almost double. Bake at 350° approximately 25-35 minutes.

-Charlene Miller

Anadama Bread

1/2 c. yellow cornmeal
2 Tbsp. butter
1/2 c. molasses
2 tsp. salt

2 c. water, boiling
1 pkg. active dry yeast
5 1/2-6 c. all-
   purpose flour

Combine cornmeal, butter, molasses, and salt in a large bowl. Add water and stir until butter is melted. Let cool until luke-warm (105°-110°). Add the yeast. Using a wooden spoon, stir in as much flour as you can. Turn out onto a lightly floured surface. Knead in enough of the remaining flour to make a moderately stiff dough that is smooth and elastic. Transfer to a greased bowl, turning once to grease dough. Cover and let rise until double, approximately 1 hour. Punch dough down. Divide dough in half, shape into 2 loaves and place in greased 8"x4" loaf pans (or shape into 2, 5" loaves and place on greased cookie sheets; flatten slightly to 6" rounds). Cover and let rise again until nearly double, approximately 30 minutes. Bake at 375° for 30 minutes, or until bread sounds hollow when you tap the top. Yield: 2 loaves

-D Brown

Bread Rolls

4 c. whole wheat flour
4 c. all-purpose flour
6 Tbsp. margarine,
   shortening or oil

4 pkg. yeast
2 tsp. salt
3 c. water, warm

Mix ingredients together. Let rise until double. Shape into buns and let rise until double in size. Bake at 350° until golden brown. Yield: large bunch of rolls or buns. NOTE: Can also take a small amount of dough and stretch it out and wrap it around a stick and bake it over an open fire, like a hot dog.

-John and Tone Kaufman, Norway

Russian Dill and Onion Bread

2 pkg. dry yeast
1/2 c. water, warm
2 c. small curd cottage
  cheese, warm
2 Tbsp. onion flakes, dried
1/2 tsp. baking soda
2 eggs

2 Tbsp. butter, melted
4 Tbsp. sugar
2-3 Tbsp. dill weed
  dried
2 tsp. salt
4 1/2 - 5 c. flour
Cornmeal

EGG WASH:
1 egg yolk

2 Tbsp. water

Dissolve yeast in warm water. Add remaining ingredients together except flour and cornmeal. Mix well. Add flour, 1 cup at a time, and blend well. Knead until smooth and elastic. Place dough in large bowl. Cover and let rise (in draft-free place) until double; punch down and let rise again. Punch down, knead well. Shape into 2 round loaves. Place on baking sheets sprinkled with cornmeal. Let loaves rise until double in size. In a small bowl, combine egg yolk with water; mix well. Gently brush loaves with egg wash. Bake at 350° for 40-50 minutes. Serves a large group.

-Charlene Miller

Lowfat Corn Bread

1 c. flour
1 c. cornmeal
1/4 c. sugar
4 tsp. baking powder

Dash of salt
1 c. milk, skim or 1%
2 egg whites
1/4 c. applesauce

Stir ingredients together. Bake at 450° in an 8"x8" pan, for 15 - 20 minutes or until golden brown.

-Carol Beachy

Lebanese Bread

3 1/2 - 4 c. flour
2 tsp. salt
1 pkg. yeast
1 1/2 c. tap water, warm

1 egg, beaten
Sesame seeds
1 tsp. water, cold

Mix 1 c. flour, salt and yeast. Gradually add water. Beat for 2 minutes. Add 3/4 c. flour. Beat at high speed for 2 minutes. Stir in enough flour to make a stiff dough. Turn onto lightly floured surface. Knead until smooth and elastic (approximately 5 minutes). Divide dough into 8 equal pieces. Roll each piece into a 5" circle. Cover and let rest on a lightly floured surface for 45 minutes. Place circles, bottom side up, on a lightly floured baking sheet. Blend egg and cold water. Brush this mixture lightly on top of each circle of dough. Sprinkle each with about 1 tsp. sesame seeds. Bake at 500° for 8 - 10 minutes or until lightly browned. Remove and cool. Cut into halves or fourths to serve. NOTE: This bread can be used for pocket sandwiches or a snack bread with cheese.

-Erma Yoder

Cheese Garlic Biscuits

2 c. Bisquick mix
2/3 c. milk
1/4 c. margarine, melted

1/4 tsp. garlic powder
3/4 c. cheddar cheese,
   shredded

Mix Bisquick, milk and cheese until soft dough forms. Beat vigorously for 30 seconds. Drop by the spoonful onto ungreased cookie sheet. Bake at 450° for 8 - 10 minutes or until golden brown. Mix margarine and garlic powder. Brush over biscuits before removing from cookie sheet. Serve warm. Yield: 10-12 biscuits.

-Angie Gerber

Oatmeal Bread

1 c. quick-cooking oatmeal
1/2 c. whole wheat
  bread flour
1/2 c. brown sugar
1 Tbsp. wheat germ
1 Tbsp. soy flour
1 Tbsp. salt

2 Tbsp. margarine
  or oil
2 Tbsp. yeast
2 c. water, hot
  (120°-130°)
4-5 c. bread flour

Place ingredients in large bowl, except the hot water and bread flour. Then pour hot water over and let set 1-2 minutes. Beat on low with hand beater for 2 minutes. By hand stir in the bread flour. Turn out on floured board and knead until smooth. Place in greased bowl. Set in a warm place to rise until double in bulk. Turn out on floured board. Divide into 2 loaves and place in greased bread pans. Let rise to top of pan then bake at 350° for 45 minutes.

-Rita Gerber

Pizza Crust

1 Tbsp. yeast
1 c. water, warm
1 Tbsp. sugar

1 tsp. salt
2 Tbsp. oil
2 1/2 c. flour

Dissolve yeast in warm water. Whisk together sugar, salt and flour. Add water and oil. Gently knead and add flour as needed. Let rise about 5 minutes (optional). Spread out on pan and add toppings. You may substitute 1 cup of flour for whole wheat flour. For toppings you can add salsa with the pizza sauce along with some oregano. Bake at 375°-400° for 15-20 minutes. Yield: 8 medium slices

-Karen Bear

Great Bread

1/3 c. brown sugar
1/3 c. honey
1-2 tsp. salt
3 Tbsp. flour
1 c. water, boiling
2 c. water, cold

2 Tbsp. yeast
3/4 c. vegetable oil
1 Tbsp. wheat gluten
1 Tbsp. dough
  enhancer
8 1/4 c. bread flour

Mix brown sugar, honey, salt, flour, and waters. Sprinkle yeast over mixture in bowl and stir in. Let rise until bubbly. Beat with whisk, adding about 2 c. bread flour. Add gluten, dough enhancer, and 3 c. bread flour. Knead, then add oil and remaining flour. If necessary add more flour until dough does not stick to sides of bowl. Let dough rest 20 minutes. Place into 3 greased loaf pans; let rise approximately 45 minutes-1 hour. Bake at 350° for 25 minutes or until golden brown. NOTE: Flour can be whole wheat or you can mix oatmeal with white flour, barley and nuts. Whatever you want.

-Mandy Beachy

Feather Light Muffins

1/3 c. shortening
1 c. sugar
1 egg
1 1/2 c. flour
1 1/2 tsp. baking powder

1/4 tsp. nutmeg
1/2 c. milk
1/2 c. butter, melted
1 tsp. cinnamon

Cream shortening, 1/2 c. sugar and egg together. In a separate bowl, combine flour, baking powder and nutmeg. Add to creamed mixture, alternating with milk. Fill greased muffin tins and bake at 325° for 20-25 minutes. Combine remaining sugar and cinnamon. To coat, roll muffins in butter and then in cinnamon mixture. Yield: 12 muffins

-Pam Buss

PTL Pumpkin Muffins

1 c. cooking oil
1 c. water
2 1/2 c. pumpkin
4 eggs
1 Tbsp. cloves
1 Tbsp. cinnamon
1 Tbsp. nutmeg
1 tsp. salt

1 3/4 tsp. baking soda
1/2 tsp. baking powder
2 3/4 c. sugar
4 c. flour
1/2 box raisins
3/4 c. walnuts,
    chopped

Mix oil, water, pumpkin and eggs together well. Mix cloves, cinnamon, nutmeg, salt, baking soda, baking powder, sugar and flour into pumpkin mixture. Add raisins and walnuts. Fill cupcake pans almost full and bake at 375° approximately 15 minutes or until they come out of the pan easily. Yield: approximately 3 1/2 dozen.

-Doris Fath

Grandma's Buns

1 Tbsp. salt
1/4 c. vegetable oil
1/2 c. + 1 tsp. sugar
2 c. tap water, very hot

2 pkg. yeast
1/2 c. water, warm
2 eggs, well beaten
6-7 c. flour

Mix salt, oil, 1/2 c. sugar and hot water. Let stand. Stir the yeast, warm water and 1 tsp. sugar and let stand until dissolved (approximately 5 minutes). Add yeast mixture to first 4 ingredients; add eggs. Add flour, 1 c. at a time, stirring well after each addition. Place into a large bowl and refrigerate. Work out 3 1/2 hours before needed. You may also use it right away, but let it rise until doubled then knead it down. Roll into walnut size balls. Put 3 balls into each muffin tin. Let rise. Bake at 350° for 15-20 minutes. Serves 2 1/2-3 dozen people.

-Charlene Miller

Nutty Rhubarb Muffins

3/4 c. brown sugar
1/3 c. vegetable oil
1 egg, beaten
1/2 c. buttermilk
1 tsp. vanilla

1/2 tsp. salt
1/2 tsp. baking soda
2 c. flour
1 c. rhubarb, diced
1/2 c. pecans, chopped

TOPPING:
1/4 c. brown sugar
1/4 c. pecans

1/2 tsp. cinnamon

Stir brown sugar and oil together in a large bowl. Stir egg into mixture. Add buttermilk and vanilla. Mix. Add salt, baking soda and flour. Mix well. Stir in rhubarb and pecans. Place into greased muffin tins. Mix topping ingredients together and sprinkle on top of muffins. Bake at 375° for 20 minutes. Yield: 12 muffins.

-Sharon Gerber

Blueberry Muffins

2 c. all-purpose flour, sifted
2 1/2 tsp. baking powder
2 Tbsp. sugar
3/4 tsp. salt

1/2 c. shortening
1 egg, well beaten
3/4 c. milk
1 c. blueberries

Mix flour, baking powder, sugar and salt in mixing bowl. Cut in shortening until crumbs are the size of peas. Make a hole in the center. In a separate bowl, combine egg and milk. Add to hole in dry ingredients. Stir only until dry ingredients are just moist (batter will be lumpy). Quickly fold in blueberries. Fill greased muffin pan cups 2/3 full or use baking tins. Bake at 400° for 25 minutes or until done. Yield: 12 muffins

-Eunice Herman

Blueberry Muffins

2 1/3 c. flour
1 1/4 c. sugar
1 1/2 tsp. baking powder
3/4 tsp. baking soda
1/4 tsp. salt
1/4 tsp. nutmeg
1/8 tsp. ground cloves

1 orange
2 eggs
1/2 c. vegetable oil
1 1/4 c. buttermilk
1/2 tsp. vanilla
1 1/2 c. blueberries

In a large bowl, combine flour, sugar, baking powder, baking soda, salt, nutmeg and cloves. Grate orange rind and stir into dry ingredients. In a small bowl, combine eggs, oil, buttermilk and vanilla. Gently stir in blueberries. Add to dry ingredients and stir until dry ingredients are moistened. Fill lightly greased or lined muffin pans 3/4 full. Bake for 18-20 minutes or until tops are lightly browned. Serves 10-12 people.

-Alma Spires

Cinnamon Pull-Aparts

20 frozen dough buns
1 c. brown sugar, packed
1 Tbsp. cinnamon
7 1/2 Tbsp. vanilla
  pudding powder (not instant)

1/2 c. raisins
1/3 c. pecans or
  walnuts, chopped
1/3 c. margarine, hard
2 Tbsp. light corn syrup

Arrange frozen buns in greased 12 cup bundt pan. In a mixing bowl, combine brown sugar, cinnamon, pudding powder, raisins and nuts. Sprinkle over buns. Melt margarine and corn syrup together in small saucepan until melted. Drizzle over sugar mixture on buns. Cover with wet tea towel. Let stand for 7-8 hours or overnight. Dough should be double in size. Bake at 350° for approximately 25 minutes. Let stand for 5 minutes. Turn out onto plate. Yield: 20 buns

-Becky Yerian

Baked French Toast

1 loaf French bread,
  cut into 1" slices
2 c. milk
2 tsp. vanilla

1/2 tsp. cinnamon
8 eggs
2 c. Half & Half
1/2 tsp. nutmeg

TOPPING:
3/4 c. butter, softened
3 Tbsp. corn syrup

1 1/3 c. brown sugar
1 c. pecans, chopped

Heavily butter 9"x13" pan. Fill pan with bread slices. Blend eggs, milk, Half & Half, vanilla, nutmeg and cinnamon. Pour mixture over bread slices. Cover and refrigerate overnight. Make topping by combining butter, corn syrup, brown sugar and pecans. Set aside. When ready to bake, spread topping over toast. Bake at 350° for 50 minutes, until puffed and golden brown. Serves 8-10 people.

-Ruth Weaver

Creamed Eggs & Biscuits

6 eggs, hard-boiled
6 Tbsp. flour
3 c. milk
6 Tbsp. butter

1 1/2 tsp. salt
Dash of pepper
Ham or bacon,
  chopped (optional)

Melt butter in a heavy saucepan. Add flour and salt, stirring until well blended. Slowly add milk and stir constantly. Cook until smooth. Chop and add eggs. Serve on toast or biscuits. Serves 6 people.

-Kathy Marner

Baked Oatmeal

3 c. instant oats
1 tsp. baking soda
2 tsp. baking powder
1/4 tsp. salt (optional)
Cinnamon (to taste)
Raisins, nuts or
  coconut (optional)

1 c. milk
1/2 c. oil
1/2 c. real maple syrup
1 tsp. vanilla
2 eggs

In a large bowl mix oats, baking soda, baking powder, salt, cinnamon and raisins. In a separate bowl beat eggs. Add milk, oil, maple syrup and vanilla. Add to oat mixture. Mix well. Bake in a 10"x10" pan at 350° for 30 minutes. NOTE: Serve warm with milk. You may add blueberries or other fruit. Very good!

-Elsie Weaver

Crustless Spinach Quiche

3 oz. cream cheese, softened
1 c. milk
4 eggs
1/4 tsp. pepper
3 c. cheddar cheese, shredded
10 oz. frozen spinach,
  thawed & drained

1 c. frozen broccoli,
  thawed & well
  drained
1 small onion, finely
  chopped
5 fresh mushrooms,
  sliced

In a bowl, beat cream cheese, add milk, eggs and pepper. Beat until smooth. Stir in remaining ingredients. Put in greased 10" quiche pan. Bake at 350° for 45 minutes until center is done. Serves 8 people.

-Carol S. Miller

Yoder's Homemade Muesli

6 c. old-fashioned oats
2 c. quick oats
3/4 c. almonds, sliced
3/4 c. walnuts, chopped

3/4 c. raisins
1/2 c. dates,
  chopped
1/4 c. honey

Mix oats, almonds and walnuts. Drizzle honey on top of mixture. Place on a cookie sheet with sides and bake at 250° for 20 minutes. Stir every 5 minutes. Remove from oven and add raisins and dates. Store in an airtight container. Serve with milk.

-Erma Yoder

Granola Cereal

6 c. rolled oats
2 c. whole wheat flour
1 c. coconut
1 c. wheat germ

1 c. sunflower seeds
1/2 c. brown sugar
1 c. raisins, dates or
  other dry fruit

BLEND TOGETHER:
1 c. honey
1 c. olive oil
1/2 c. water

2 tsp. vanilla
1 tsp. salt

In a large bowl mix oats, flour, coconut, wheat germ, sunflower seeds and brown sugar. In a separate bowl blend honey, olive oil, water, vanilla and salt. Add to dry ingredients and mix well. Spread in 2 greased cookie sheets. Bake at 250° for 1 hour or until dry and golden. Stir every 15 minutes. After granola has cooled, add raisins, dates or other dried fruit. Store in covered container.

-Dean and Arvilla Kaufman

Spinach Quiche

CRUST:

1 1/2 c. flour
4 oz. margarine
5 tsp. water, cold

1/4 c. Parmesan
  cheese, shredded

Combine flour with margarine and mix with fork until it has the consistency of crumbs. Add water and mix until it makes a ball. Place dough on a clean, floured surface. Roll dough into circle and place in a 9" pie pan. Sprinkle Parmesan cheese over pastry.

FILLING:

1 lb. fresh spinach,
  cooked and drained
3 eggs, beaten
1 c. cottage cheese
1 c. cream
1/4 c. onion,
  finely chopped

1 1/2 tsp. salt
1/4 tsp. nutmeg
1/4 tsp. pepper
1/4 tsp. salsa
1 Tbsp. butter

Cut spinach and discard stems. Cook spinach and drain well. Combine eggs, cottage cheese, cream, onion, salt, nutmeg, pepper and salsa. Mix well and combine with spinach. Place mixture into pie pastry. Place butter on mixture. Bake at 350° for 25-30 minutes, until center of pie is firm.

-Betty Müller, Colombia

Baked Breakfast Burritos

6-8 bacon strips
8 fresh mushrooms, sliced
Onions, sliced (to taste)
1/3 c. green peppers,
  chopped
1 garlic clove, minced
8 eggs
1/4 c. cheddar or Monterey
  Jack cheese, shredded

3 Tbsp. enchilada or
  taco sauce
1 Tbsp. butter or
  margarine
4 large flour tortillas
  (ginches)
Sour cream
Enchilada or
  taco sauce, optional

In a skillet, cook bacon until crisp. Place on a paper towel to drain. Reserve 1 Tbsp. of the drippings. Saute mushrooms, onions, green peppers and garlic in drippings until tender. Set aside and keep warm. In a bowl, beat eggs and sour cream together. Stir in cheese and enchilada sauce. In the skillet, melt butter and add egg mixture. Cook over low heat, stirring occasionally until eggs are set. Remove from heat. Crumble the bacon. Combine bacon, egg mixture and mushroom mixture together. Spoon down center of tortillas, roll up, place seam side down, in an 11"x7" baking dish. Sprinkle cheese on the top. Bake at 350° for 5 minutes or until cheese melts. Serve with sour cream and enchilada sauce. Serves 4 people.

-Elsie Schrock

"We are made kind by being kind."
-Eric Hoffer

Whole Wheat Buttermilk Pancakes

1 c. buttermilk
2 Tbsp. vegetable oil
1 egg
1/2 c. whole wheat flour
1/2 c. white flour,
  unbleached

1 tsp. baking powder
1/2 tsp. baking soda
1/2 tsp. salt

Combine buttermilk, oil and egg in a bowl and mix with a fork or wire whisk. Add flours, baking powder, baking soda and salt. Stir and mix until moistened. Fry in hot, lightly greased skillet. Serve with your favorite toppings. Serves 3 people. NOTE: Unbleached, white flour can be substituted with part soy flour and wheat germ.

-Alma Spires

Brunch Pizza Squares

1 lb. pork sausage, bulk
8 oz. refrigerated crescent
  rolls
4 eggs

2 Tbsp. milk
1/8 tsp. pepper
3/4 c. cheddar
  cheese

Fry sausage in a pan and drain. Unroll crescent rolls. Place in a lightly greased 13"x9" pan. Press dough 1/2" up sides, seal seams, sprinkle with sausage. In a bowl, beat eggs, milk and pepper. Pour over sausage. Sprinkle with cheese. Bake uncovered at 400° for 15 minutes, until crust is brown and cheese is melted. Serves 8 people.

-Carol S. Miller

Fajita Omelette

1 boneless, skinless
  chicken breast
1/2 tsp. vegetable oil
1/2 tsp. lime juice
1/4 tsp. chili powder
1/8 tsp. salt
1/8 tsp. cumin
Dash garlic powder
Dash black pepper
1/2 c. green bell pepper, diced

1/2 c. medium Spanish
  onion, diced
1/2 c. tomato, diced
2 tsp. butter
5 large eggs, beaten
1 c. cheddar cheese,
  shredded
1/3 c. salsa
2 Tbsp. sour cream

Pound the chicken breast between sheets of plastic wrap until about 1/4" thick. Cut the meat into bite-size pieces. Pour oil into a medium skillet over high heat. Add the meat and saute it for a few minutes until it browns. Add the lime juice to meat. Blend the spices together in a small bowl. Then add this mixture to meat. Mix well until blended. Add pepper and onion to meat and simmer for 5-10 minutes over medium heat or until vegetables begin to brown. Add tomato and cook another 2 minutes. Set a large skillet over medium heat. Add 1 tsp. of butter to the pan. When butter has melted add half of the beaten eggs to the pan and swirl to coat entire bottom of pan. Cook eggs for 1 minute until top surface begins to firm. Be sure bottom is not getting too brown before top cooks. If you notice this is happening turn the heat down. Sprinkle about 1/4 c. cheese down the center of eggs. Spoon a heaping Tbsp. of salsa over cheese. Spoon 1/4 of meat and vegetables onto salsa. Fold edges over center of omelette and let it cook for approximately 1 minute. Carefully flip omelette over in pan with seam down. Let it cook for 1 or 2 minutes. Slide it out onto a serving plate. Keep this in the oven at 300° while you prepare the other one. When both omelettes are done, spoon remaining meat and vegetables over omelettes. Sprinkle a couple Tbsp. of cheese over toppings. Add 2 Tbsp. of salsa. Serves 2 people.

-Marlin Yoder

Salads and
Salad Dressings

Tabooley
Cracked Wheat and Parsley Salad

Water
3/4 c. cracked wheat (bulgur)
1 1/2 c. parsley, snipped
3 medium tomatoes, chopped
1/3 c. green onions, chopped
2 Tbsp. fresh mint, snipped or
 2 tsp. mint, dried and crushed

1/4 c. olive oil
1/4 c. lemon juice
1 tsp. salt
1/4 tsp. pepper
olives, ripe
 (if desired)

Cover cracked wheat with cold water; let stand 30 minutes. Drain and press out as much water as possible. Place wheat, parsley, tomatoes, green onions and mint in glass bowl. In a separate bowl mix olive oil, lemon juice, salt and pepper. Pour over wheat mixture and toss. Cover and refrigerate at least 1 hour. Garnish with olives. NOTE: This recipe is from Nepal.

-Tammy Koser

Spinach Salad

1 bag spinach, washed and
 drained (not stems)
1 c. fresh mushrooms, sliced
2 hard-boiled eggs, chopped
 or sliced

4 slices bacon, fried
 crisp, crumbled
Colby or other cheese,
 shredded or cubed

DRESSING:
3/4 c. sugar
3/4 c. salad oil
1 small onion, chopped
1/3 c. ketchup

1 tsp. salt
1/4 c. vinegar
1 tsp. Worcestershire
 sauce

Toss spinach, mushrooms, eggs, bacon and cheese together. Mix dressing ingredients together, but wait to put it on salad until ready to serve.

-Doris Fath

Spinach Salad

1 lb. spinach
8 slices bacon
1 can bean sprouts
3 hard-boiled eggs, chopped

1 c. cheddar cheese,
shredded

DRESSING:
1/2 c. vegetable oil
3/4 c. sugar
1/3 c. ketchup
1/4 c. vinegar
1 Tbsp. Worcestershire sauce

Dash of salt
1 medium onion,
finely chopped

Wash and drain spinach. Fry bacon and crumble. Drain bean sprouts. Mix spinach, bacon, bean sprouts, eggs and cheese together. Combine dressing ingredients together in shaker and shake well. Mix salad and dressing together. Chill before serving. Serves 4-6 people.

-Sharon Gerber

Taco Salad

1 lb. ground beef
1 pkg. Taco Bell seasoning
1 head of lettuce
8 oz. Velveeta cheese,
shredded

1 jar Hartville Kitchen
French Salad
Dressing
3/4 of a 14 oz. bag
Doritos, crushed

Brown ground beef, drain and stir in seasoning. Cool. Mix lettuce and Velveeta cheese together and add to ground beef. Stir in dressing and crushed Doritos.

-Kathy Torrence

53

Frito Salad

1 head lettuce, torn into
bite size pieces
30 oz. kidney beans,
washed and drained
1-2 lbs. Longhorn
cheese, shredded

l regular size bag
Fritos, crumbled
1 jar Hartville
Kitchen French
Salad Dressing

Mix lettuce, beans and cheese together. When ready to serve add Fritos and dressing.

-Louise Marner

Dandelion Salad

2 hard-boiled eggs,
sliced and cooled
2 slices bacon, chopped
4 Tbsp. flour
1 tsp. salt

3 Tbsp. sugar
3 Tbsp. vinegar
1 1/2 c. water or milk
4 c. dandelion
greens, chopped

Place dandelion greens in a bowl. Fry bacon until crisp. Leave 2 Tbsp. bacon grease in skillet with bacon. Combine flour, salt, sugar, vinegar and water, then add to skillet. Cook, stirring constantly, until sauce is smooth and thick. Pour the sauce over dandelion greens and toss. Garnish with eggs and bacon bits. Serves 4-6 people. NOTE: Gather dandelions very early in the spring before buds develop. With a small sharp knife gather entire plants. Cut off leaves, wash carefully, drain and chop.

-Alma Spires

Overnight Lettuce Salad

1 head lettuce, broken up
1 head cauliflower,
 finely chopped
1 sweet onion, chopped

1 lb. bacon, fried and
 crumbled
1/3 c. Parmesan or
 mozzarella cheese

DRESSING:
2 c. Miracle Whip

1/4 c. sugar

Mix Miracle Whip and sugar together. Layer lettuce, cauliflower, onion and bacon in that order. Spread dressing on top and sprinkle with cheese. Seal and refrigerate overnight to season. Toss just before serving. This is a family favorite. Serves 10-12 people.

-Donna Weaver

Chinese Coleslaw

2 pkg. coleslaw mix
1 c. almonds, sliced
5 Tbsp. sesame seeds
2 Tbsp. butter

1 bunch green
 onions, chopped
2 pkg. Ramen noodles

DRESSING:
1 1/2 c. salad oil
9 Tbsp. vinegar
6 Tbsp. sugar

3 tsp. salt
1/2 tsp. pepper

Mix dressing ingredients and set aside. Brown almonds and sesame seeds in butter. Cool. Combine cabbage mix and onions in large bowl. Add almonds, sesame seeds and dressing then toss. Break noodles into small pieces and discard seasonings. Add noodles just before serving.

-Carol Miller

Chinese Cabbage Salad

1 small head cabbage, shredded
1/2 c. almonds, slivered
1-2 Tbsp. butter

5 oz. Ramen noodles,
uncooked and light-
ly crushed

SAUCE:
Ramen noodle seasoning pkg.
1/4 c. olive oil

1/4 c. soy sauce
1/4 c. sugar

Toast almonds and noodles in butter. Place cabbage in a large bowl. Combine sauce ingredients in a separate bowl and mix well. Blend in almonds and noodles. Just before serving, pour mixture over cabbage. NOTE: Does not keep well.

-Carol Yoder

Apple-Cabbage Slaw

1 1/2 tsp. lemon juice
(optional)
2 c. apples, sliced

3 c. cabbage,
shredded

DRESSING:
1/2 c. sour cream
or plain yogurt
2 tsp. honey
1/2 tsp. salt
1 Tbsp. vinegar

1/2 tsp. prepared
mustard
1/2 tsp. pepper
(optional)

Mix sour cream, honey, salt, mustard, pepper and vinegar together. Sprinkle lemon juice over apples to prevent darkening. Mix apples and cabbage together. Pour dressing over mixture and toss lightly.

-Rachel Keim

Celery Seed Slaw

3 lb. cabbage, coarsely
  shredded
1/2 c. carrots, finely
  shredded
1/2 c. green pepper,
  chopped

1 c. sugar
1 c. vinegar
1 Tbsp. salt
1 tsp. celery seed

In a large bowl, combine cabbage, carrots and peppers. In a saucepan, combine sugar, vinegar, salt, and celery seed. Bring to a boil. Pour over cabbage mixture and toss. Cover and refrigerate 4 hours or overnight. Serves 12-16 people.

-Erma Yoder

Deluxe Broccoli-Cauliflower Salad

1 head cauliflower
1 bundle broccoli
1/2 lb. bacon, fried
  and crumbled

2 c. cheddar cheese,
  grated
1 c. raisins
1/2 c. sunflower seeds

DRESSING:
1 c. Miracle Whip
1/4 c. sugar

2 Tbsp. vinegar
1/4 tsp. salt

Cut broccoli and cauliflower into bite size pieces. Combine bacon, raisins, cheese and sunflower seeds; add to broccoli. Mix dressing ingredients together. Stir into broccoli mixture. Refrigerate.

-Angie Peck

Oriental Chicken Salad

2 c. chicken, cooked
   and shredded
1 bag cabbage, shredded
1 c. sunflower seeds,
   shelled

1/2 c. almonds,
   slivered
2 pkg. chicken
   flavored Ramen
   noodles, uncooked
   and crumbled

DRESSING:
1/2 c. olive oil
3 Tbsp. vinegar
3 Tbsp. sugar
Salt (to taste)

Seasoning
   packs from Ramen
   noodles
Pepper (to taste)

*Mix chicken, cabbage, sunflower seeds, almonds and noodles
together. In a separate bowl, combine dressing ingredients
and pour over salad. Mix well.*

-Teresea Morris

Sweet Chicken Salad

16 oz. chicken,
  boneless and diced
3/4 c. mayonnaise
1 stalk celery, finely diced
1 Tbsp. sweet pickle
  relish
1/2 tsp. garlic salt
Dash of pepper

Combine mayonnaise and chicken. Sprinkle with garlic salt and pepper. Add celery and relish. Mix well. Serve on sandwiches or with crackers.

-Kathy Torrence

"The dedicated life is the life worth living."
-Annie Dillard-

Pasta Salad

1 box pasta shells,
  medium size
1 box Rainbow
  spiral pasta
2 cans black olives, sliced
1 can green olives, sliced
1 red onion, chopped
4 tomatoes, chopped
1/4 lb. mozzarella
  cheese, grated
1/4 lb. pepperoni,
  chopped
1/2 c. oil
1/3 c. white vinegar
1 Tbsp. oregano

Cook pastas and let cool. Add remaining ingredients and chill in refrigerator at least 3 hours or overnight. NOTE: If desired, you can add more oil and vinegar.

-Esther Yoder

Sweet & Sour Pasta Salad

1 box mixed vegetables,
  frozen
1 c. macaroni, cooked
1/3 c. onion, chopped

2 c. celery, diced
1 can red kidney beans
1/2 c. green pepper,
  chopped

DRESSING:
1/2 c. vinegar
1 tsp. salt
1 egg, beaten
1 Tbsp. flour

1 c. sugar
1 tsp. prepared mustard
1 tsp. celery seed
1 Tbsp. butter

Cook and drain vegetables. Rinse and drain kidney beans. Combine kidney beans and macaroni with vegetables. Mix dressing ingredients together with wire whip. Cook until thickened. Pour over vegetables while hot. Let stand for several hours or overnight. Serves 6-10 people.

-Eunice Herman

Grandma's Potato Salad

12 c. potatoes, cooked & diced
12 hard-boiled eggs, sliced

1 c. celery, chopped
1 onion, chopped

DRESSING:
3 c. salad dressing
4 tsp. salt
1/4 c. vinegar

4 Tbsp. mustard
1 3/4 c. sugar
1/2 c. milk

Combine potatoes, eggs, celery and onion. Mix dressing ingredients together and let stand for a half hour. Mix dressing with potato mixture and refrigerate until ready to serve. Serves 25 people.

-Naomi Gingerich

Chicken Pasta Salad

4 c. rotelli pasta, cooked,
  drained and rinsed
2 c. chicken breast,
  cooked and cubed
1 c. water chestnuts, sliced

1/2 c. parsley,
  chopped
1/2 c. green onions,
  chopped
8 c. spinach, torn

DRESSING:
1/4 c. sesame seed
1/4 c. oil
1/8 c. soy sauce
1/3 c. white vinegar

3 Tbsp. sugar
Salt (to taste)
Pepper (to taste)

Mix pasta, chicken, water chestnuts and parsley in a large bowl. To make dressing, warm sesame seed in 1-2 Tbsp. of oil. Cool. Mix with remaining dressing ingredients. Pour most of the marinade dressing over the chicken mixture. Save a little dressing to add at serving time to prevent dryness. Marinate all but onions and spinach overnight. When ready to serve, add spinach, onions and remaining dressing. Toss and serve. Serves 6 people.

-Erma Yoder

Sweet & Sour Dressing

2 1/2 c. sugar
1/2 c. Miracle Whip
3/4 c. vinegar
1/4 c. mustard

1/2 tsp. celery seed
1/2 c. salad oil
1/2 tsp. black pepper
1 Tbsp. minced onion

Mix ingredients together until well blended. Refrigerate.

-Kathy Marner

Potato Salad

12 c. potatoes, cooked
  and sliced
12 eggs, cooked and mashed

1/2 medium onion,
  chopped
1 1/2 c. celery, diced

DRESSING:
3 c. Miracle Whip
2 tsp. salt
2 1/2 c. sugar

1/4 c. vinegar
6 Tbsp. mustard
1/2 c. milk

Combine potatoes, eggs, onions and celery. Mix dressing ingredients and pour over potato mixture, stirring well. NOTE: Tastes better when mixed 1 or 2 days ahead of serving. Serves 30-40 people.

-Edna Weaver

Ukrainian Potato Salad

3 medium potatoes,
  finely diced and boiled
1 medium onion, diced
1/2 lb. summer sausage,
  diced (optional)
3-4 hard-boiled eggs, diced
3-4 crunchy dill pickle
  spears, diced

2-3 medium carrots,
  diced and cooked
1 1/2 c. peas,
  cooked and drained
1/4 tsp. black pepper
1/4 tsp. salt
3 Tbsp. Hellman's
  mayonnaise

Toss all ingredients together. Serves 5-6 people.

-Nadia Lotut

Nutty Fruit Salad

4 large red apples, chopped
2 c. green grapes
2 medium bananas (firm), sliced
1 c. walnuts, chopped
1/2 c. mayonnaise

4 Tbsp. sour cream
1 tsp. sugar
1 tsp. lemon juice
1/2 tsp. salt

In a large bowl, combine apples, grapes, bananas and walnuts. In a separate bowl, combine mayonnaise, sour cream, sugar, lemon juice and salt. Pour over fruit mixture and toss to coat. Serves 8-12 people.

-Carol S. Miller

Waldorf Salad

3-4 apples, chopped
with peeling on
2 c. grapes, seedless
and halved
1 c. celery, finely chopped
4 bananas, sliced

1/2 c. walnuts,
chopped
20 oz. pineapple
tidbits
1/2 c. cream
1 tsp. vanilla

DRESSING:
1 c. water
1 c. sugar
1/4 tsp. salt

1 tsp. vinegar
1 Tbsp. cornstarch

In a saucepan, mix water, sugar, salt, vinegar and cornstarch to make dressing. Boil until thickened. Cool. Add cream and vanilla. Mix fruit together in separate bowl. Add walnuts and dressing to fruit just before serving. Serves 8 people.

-Kathy Marner

Waldorf Salad

2 c. pineapple tidbits
1 c. pineapple juice
2 c. grapes, halved
6 apples, cored
  but not peeled

1/4 c. nuts
2/3 c. sugar
2 Tbsp. cornstarch
1/2 tsp. salt
1 egg, beaten

Bring pineapple juice to a boil. In a bowl, mix sugar, corn-starch and salt together. Add egg and blend. Combine this mixture with the hot pineapple juice and cook over low heat until thoroughly cooked, but do not overcook. Cool. Cut apples into small chunks (both red and yellow apples look nice). Mix pineapple, apples, grapes and nuts together. Pour cooked mixture over the fruit. Keep refrigerated.

-Elsie Schrock

French Dressing

1 medium onion
3/4 c. sugar
2 Tbsp. Worcestershire sauce
1 tsp. salt

1 c. vegetable oil
1/2 c. ketchup
1/4 c. vinegar

Place all ingredients together in a blender and blend until smooth.

-Malinda Yoder

Creamy Garlic Dressing

1 1/2 c. mayonnaise
3/4 c. canola oil
1/4 c. vinegar

3 Tbsp. onion, chopped
1 Tbsp. garlic, minced
1 1/2 tsp. sugar

Place all ingredients in a blender and mix until smooth. Yield: 3 cups.

-Carol S. Miller

"You don't just luck into things...You build
step by step, whether it's friendships
or opportunities." -Barbara Bush

Celery Seed Salad Dressing

1 onion, chopped
1 c. sugar
1 1/2 tsp. salt
1/2 c. vinegar

1 c. vegetable oil
1 1/2 tsp. mustard
1 1/2 tsp. celery seed

Mix ingredients together in blender. Refrigerate. Enjoy on your lettuce salads.

-Alma Spires

Ranch Dip or Dressing

1 c. sour cream
1 c. mayonnaise
1 garlic clove, minced
1 Tbsp. parsley

2 tsp. dill
Dash of seasoned
    salt
1/2 tsp. paprika
1/2 - 3/4 c. buttermilk

To make as a dip, mix sour cream, mayonnaise, garlic, parsley, dill, salt and paprika. For a salad dressing, mix these ingredients and add buttermilk. NOTE: If you don't have buttermilk, add 1 tsp. vinegar or lemon juice to 1 c. milk.

-Mandy Beachy

Cranberry Salad

1 large box red jello
1 bag cranberries, chopped
1/2 c. pecans, chopped
2 bananas, mashed

2 apples, chopped
1 c. sugar
3 c. water

Bring 2 c. water to a boil. Add sugar and bring to a boil again. Remove from heat; add jello and 1 c. water. Add remaining ingredients and mix. Refrigerate overnight.

-Erma Yoder

Cranberry Waldorf Salad

2 c. raw cranberries
3 c. mini marshmallows
3/4 c. sugar
1 1/2 c. grapes

1/4 tsp. salt
1/2 c. walnuts
2 c. apples, diced
1 c. cream

Grind cranberries. Combine with marshmallows and sugar. Refrigerate overnight. Add grapes, salt, walnuts and apples. Fold in cream. Serves 6-8 people.

-Kathy Marner

Festive Cranberry Salad

14 oz. sweetened
  condensed milk
1/4 c. lemon juice
20 oz. crushed
  pineapple, drained
16 oz. whole-berry
  cranberry sauce

2 c. miniature
  marshmallows
1/2 cup pecans,
  chopped
8 oz. whipped
  topping

In a bowl, combine milk and lemon juice; mix well. Stir in the pineapple, cranberry sauce, marshmallows and pecans. Fold in whipped topping. Spoon into a 13"x9"x2" baking dish. Freeze until firm; at least 4 hours or overnight. Cut into squares and serve.

-Marjorie Weiss

Christmas Salad

3 oz. strawberry jello
3 oz. lemon jello
3 oz. lime jello
1 can cranberry sauce
1 oz. cream cheese
1 small can crushed
  pineapple, undrained

1/4 c. walnuts, crushed
8 oz. pears, chopped
  and undrained
1 1/2 c. water

Dissolve strawberry jello in 1/4 c. water. Add cranberry sauce and pour into mold. Chill until set. Then dissolve lemon jello in 1/4 c. water. Whip cream cheese until smooth and add to jello. Stir in pineapple and walnuts. Pour on top of first layer and chill until set up. Then dissolve lime jello in 1 c. boiling water. Add pears; pour on top of second layer. Chill until firm.

-Mrs. Evelyn Mills (First Baptist Church, Dover, OH)

Molded Chef's Salad

6 oz. lemon or lime jello
2 tsp. salt
2 c. water, boiling
1 c. water, cold
3 Tbsp. vinegar
3/4 c. ham strips,
  cooked and sliced thin

3/4 c. Swiss cheese
  strips, sliced thin
1/4 c. scallions,
  sliced or red onion
1/2 green pepper,
  cut into thin strips

Dissolve jello and salt in boiling water. Add cold water and vinegar. Chill until thickened. Fold in remaining ingredients. Pour into a 5 c. jello mold. Chill until firm, at least 6 hours. Unmold. Garnish if desired. Serve with mayonnaise. Serves 5-6 people.

-Lois Smith

Jazzy Gelatin

6 oz. orange gelatin
2 c. water, boiling
1 c. ice cubes
15 oz. mandarin
  oranges, drained
1 c. grapes (optional)

1 can unsweetened
  pineapple, undrained
1 can frozen concen-
  trated orange juice,
  thawed

In a bowl, dissolve gelatin in water. Add ice cubes, oranges, pineapple and orange juice. Pour into a 6 c. mold. Refrigerate until firm. Unmold. Before serving fill center with grapes. Serves 12 people.

-Carol S. Miller

Holiday Cranberry Mousse

6 oz. cherry jello
1 c. water, boiling
16 oz. cranberry sauce
3 Tbsp. lemon juice
1 tsp. lemon peel, grated
1/2 tsp. nutmeg

20 oz. crushed
  pineapple
Pineapple juice
2 c. sour cream
1/2 c. pecans,
  chopped (optional)

Dissolve jello in water and add pineapple juice. Set aside to cool. Stir in cranberry sauce, lemon juice, lemon peel and nutmeg. Chill until thickened. Fold in pineapple, sour cream and nuts. Place in mold, if desired. Serves 8-10 people.

-Carol S. Miller

69

Picnic Rice Salad

3 c. rice, cooked & cooled
2 hard-boiled eggs, chopped
1/2 c. celery, chopped
1/3 c. green pepper, chopped
1/4 c. onion, chopped
2 oz. pimentos, diced & drained
1/4 c. dill pickle relish
1/3 c. mayonnaise

1/3 c. sweet pickle relish
1/4 c. French salad dressing
1 tsp. salt
1/4 tsp. pepper
Leaf lettuce

In a large bowl, combine rice, eggs, celery, green peppers, onions, pimentos and dill pickle relish. In a small bowl, combine mayonnaise, sweet pickle relish, salad dressing, salt and pepper. Fold into the rice mixture. Serve in a lettuce-lined bowl. Refrigerate leftovers. Serves 4-6 people.

-Dean and Arvilla Kaufman

Blueberry Salad

2 small pkg. grape or lemon jello
2 c. water, boiling
1 No. 2 can pineapple, crushed
1 can blueberry pie filling
8 oz. cream cheese

1/2 pt. sour cream
1 tsp. vanilla
1/2 c. sugar
1/2 c. nuts, chopped

Mix jello, water, pineapple and pie filling together. Chill until congealed. In a separate bowl, mix cream cheese, sour cream, sugar and vanilla together. Spread over congealed mixture and sprinkle with nuts.

-Ruth Weaver

70

Ribbon Salad

6 oz. lime jello
3 oz. lemon jello
6 oz. cherry jello
5 c. water, hot
4 c. water, cold
1/4 lb. miniature marshmallows

8 oz. cream cheese
1/2 c. pineapple,
  crushed
1 c. whipped topping

Combine lime jello, 2 c. hot water and 2 c. cold water. Pour into 9"x13" pan and chill to set. Combine lemon jello and 1 c. hot water. Add marshmallows and cream cheese. When mixture starts to set, add pineapple and whipped topping. Pour over 1st layer and chill to set. Combine cherry jello, 2 c. hot water and 2 c. cold water. When mixture starts to set, pour over 2nd layer.

-Ruth Weaver

Cream Cheese Salad

2 small pkg. orange jello
8 oz. cream cheese
1 c. pineapple, crushed

1 c. whipping cream
1 c. sugar
1 tsp. vanilla

Prepare 1 box jello and pour half into the bottom of a pan. Chill until set. Reserve remaining part of this jello for the top. Mix the other box of jello with water and cool. Add pineapple, cream cheese, whipping cream, sugar and vanilla. Pour over hardened jello and let it set. Add the remaining jello to the top.

-Ruth Weaver

"An Onion is a vegetable that can make people cry. The rest were created to make us smile."

-Betsy Leonard

Soups and
Vegetables

Savory & Spicy Vegetable Soup

46 oz. tomato juice or V8
46 oz. beef broth
46 oz. water
3 parsley sprigs, chopped
1/4 tsp. thyme
1/4 tsp. marjoram
1 small bay leaf
1/4 c. onion, chopped
1/2 c. celery with
  leaves, diced

10 peppercorns
3 cloves, whole
1 Tbsp. salt
2 bags frozen mixed
  vegetables
1 Tbsp. chili powder
2-3 Tbsp.
  Worcestershire sauce
2 rings smoked
  sausage, chopped
  (optional)

Pour tomato juice, beef broth and water into a large stockpot and bring to a boil. Simmer. Add parsley, thyme, marjoram, onion, celery and salt. Place bay leaf, peppercorns and cloves in a tea ball. Add tea ball, chili powder, Worcestershire sauce and sausage to soup. Simmer for 1-2 hours. Add frozen vegetables and simmer until vegetables are tender.

-Lynette Miller

Vegetable Soup

1 lb. ground chuck or
  beef chunks
2 1/2 c. tomato juice
2 1/2 c. water
1 tsp. chili powder
1/2 c. white sugar

1/4 c. alphabets pasta
1 large pkg. frozen
  mixed vegetables
Onion (to taste)
Salt (to taste)
Pepper (to taste)

Brown beef and onion; if using beef chunks, brown well. Mix remaining ingredients together and cook in a crockpot all day. Serves 6-8 people.

-Kathy Marner

Slow Cooker Vegetable Soup

1 lb. boneless round
  steak, cubed
3 c. water
1/2 tsp. oregano
1/2 tsp. salt
1/4 tsp. pepper
1/4 tsp. dried basil
14 1/2 oz. diced
  tomatoes, undrained

2 medium potatoes,
  cubed
2 medium onions,
  diced
2 celery ribs, sliced
2 carrots, sliced
1 1/2 c. frozen
  vegetables
3 beef bouillon cubes

*Mix ingredients together in a crockpot, except vegetables.
Cover and cook on high for 6 hours. Add vegetables. Cover
and cook on high for 2 more hours, until meat and vegetables
are tender.*

-Christina Troyer

Vegetable Cheese Chowder

1 pkg. frozen broccoli
  with cheese sauce
12 oz. corn, drained
1 sweet pepper,
  chopped

1 pkg. all veggie,
  frozen
2 1/2 c. light cream

*In a saucepan, cook broccoli, sweet pepper and frozen veg-
etable mix until tender. Add cheese sauce, corn and cream.
Cook until heated through.*

-Kathy Torrence

75

Potato Soup

6 potatoes, peeled and cut
  into bite size pieces
1-2 onions, finely chopped
1 carrot, peeled and sliced
1 stalk celery, sliced
4 chicken bouillon cubes

1 Tbsp. parsley flakes
5 c. water
1 tsp. salt
Dash of pepper
1/4-1/3 c. butter
1 can evaporated milk

Stir ingredients together in a crockpot. Cover and cook on low for 8-10 hours. If desired, mash potatoes with a masher before serving. NOTE: For variation try cheesy potato soup by stirring in 1-2 c. grated cheese before serving.

-Sara Mae Stutzman

Golden Creamy Potato Soup

4 c. potatoes, diced
1 1/2 c. water
1/2 c. celery, sliced
1/2 c. carrots, sliced
1/4 c. onions, diced
1 tsp. parsley flakes
1/2 tsp. salt

1 1/2 c. milk
2 Tbsp. flour
1/2 lb. Velveeta
  cheese, cubed
2 chicken bouillon
  cubes
Dash of pepper

In a large saucepan, combine potatoes, water, celery, carrots, onions, parsley flakes, bouillon cubes, salt and pepper. Mix well. Cover and simmer for 15-20 minutes until vegetables are tender. In a separate bowl, gradually add milk to flour, mixing well until blended. Add mixture to vegetables. Cook until thickened. Add cheese and stir until melted. Serves 6 - 8 people.

-Beth Ernst

Broccoli & Cheese Soup

3 Tbsp. butter
1 1/2 Tbsp. dry onion, scant
6 c. water
6 chicken bouillon cubes
8 oz. fine noodles

20 oz. broccoli,
  chopped (or less)
6 c. milk
1 lb. Velveeta cheese

Sauté onion in butter. Add water and bouillon cubes; heat until dissolved. Add noodles and broccoli. Cook until done, approximately 20 minutes. Add milk and cheese and heat until cheese is melted.

-Sara Mae Stutzman

Quick & Easy Cauliflower Soup

10 oz. cauliflower, frozen
1/2 c. water
21 1/2 oz. condensed
  cream of potato soup

2 c. milk
1 c. shredded Swiss
  cheese

In a 3 qt. saucepan, combine cauliflower and water. Cover and cook for 5 minutes or until tender. Do not drain. Cut larger pieces of cauliflower. Slightly mash cauliflower slightly. Add potato soup, milk and cheese. Cook, stirring, until cheese is melted and soup is heated through. Serves 4 people.

-Lois Smith

77

Ham Chowder

3 c. water
4 potatoes, diced
1 c. celery, chopped
1 c. carrots, diced and pared
1/2 c. onions, diced
2 tsp. salt
1/4 tsp. pepper

1/2 c. butter
1/2 c. flour
1 qt. milk
1 lb. Velveeta or
  cheddar cheese
2 c. ham, cubed and
  cooked

Boil vegetables in water with salt and pepper until tender. In a separate saucepan, melt butter. Add flour then milk. Stir constantly until boiling and thickened. Add vegetables with water, to sauce. Add cheese and ham; heat to boiling, stirring constantly. Serve immediately after cheese is melted.
Serves 6 people.

-Kathy Marner

Corn & Bean Soup

10 1/2 oz. chicken broth
2 medium carrots, diced
2 celery ribs, diced
1 small potato, peeled
  and diced
1 small onion, chopped
1 1/2 c. corn, frozen

15 oz. whole kidney
  beans, rinsed and
  drained
1 c. skim milk
1 tsp. dried thyme
1/4 tsp. garlic powder
Pepper (to taste)

In a large saucepan, combine broth, carrots, celery, potatoes and onions. Bring to a boil. Reduce heat; cover and simmer for 10-12 minutes or until vegetables are tender. Stir in remaining ingredients. Simmer 5-7 minutes or until corn is tender. Yield: 5 servings. NOTE: 1 serving: 185 calories; 2 grams fat; 35 grams carbohydrates; 11 grams protein.

-Joanne Weaver

Grandma's Rivel Soup

3/4 c. flour   2 Tbsp. butter
1 medium egg   2 qt. milk
1 tsp. salt

Mix flour, egg and salt together until they are very fine crumbs. In a saucepan boil butter and milk. Use a slotted spoon to stir milk constantly, while scattering crumbs (rivels) in very slowly. Bring soup back to a boil, then reduce to a simmer until thickened.

-Carol Miller

Cuban Black Bean Soup

2 c. dried black beans,   2 green peppers,
  washed   chopped
2 1/2 qt. water   4-6 garlic cloves,
2 bay leaves   pressed
1 fresh jalapeno pepper,   Salt (to taste)
  chopped   1 1/2-2 c. rice,
1/4 c. olive oil   cooked
3 large onions, chopped

Soak beans in water overnight. Drain and add enough water to cover beans. Add bay leaves and jalapeno peppers. Cover and simmer 1 1/2 - 2 hours. Sauté onions in oil approximately 3 minutes. Stir in garlic and green peppers and sauté for 1 more minute. When beans are tender add onion mixture and season with salt. Let simmer another 20 minutes. Serve over rice. Serves 4-6 people.

-Wanda Schrock

Black Bean Soup

30 oz. black beans or 1 lb.
  dry black beans,
  soaked and cooked
1 1/2 lb. bacon
2 tsp. celery salt
2 c. chicken broth
1 1/2 Tbsp. olive oil
1 1/2 c. green peppers,
  chopped

1 1/2 c. onions,
  chopped
1 1/2 Tbsp. garlic,
  minced
19 oz. tomatoes with
  juice
1/4 c. red wine vinegar
Tabasco sauce
  (optional)

Lightly brown bacon and cut into small pieces. Combine bacon with beans. Add broth and celery salt. In a separate skillet, cook peppers, onions and garlic in oil. When soft add tomatoes and vinegar. If using slab bacon, remove and discard skin. Combine ingredients together and simmer until heated through. Serve with Tabasco sauce. Can be eaten as soup or served over rice. NOTE: If using dry beans you should have about 6 c. beans and 4 c. liquid after cooking.

-Chris Bower

Chili

2 lb. hamburger
1 small onion or
  1-2 tsp. minced onion
1 can chili magic beans
  in sauce
46 oz. tomato juice

2 tsp. chili powder
1 tsp. ground red
  pepper
Any other peppers or
  hot sauce (to taste)

Brown hamburger and onion in skillet. Combine all ingredients in a large kettle. Bring to a boil. Reduce heat and simmer for 2-4 hours, stirring occasionally. NOTE: A crockpot works well too.

-John Gross

Kathy's Chili Soup

1 lb. hamburger
1 medium onion
1 qt. tomato juice
16 oz. kidney beans
16 oz. pork-n-beans
16 oz. stewed tomatoes
16 oz. whole
  tomatoes, peeled

1 Tbsp. chili powder
3 Tbsp. flour
1/3 c. water
1/4 c. brown sugar
1/4 c. ketchup

Brown hamburger and onion. Except water and flour, mix remaining ingredients together. Simmer all day in crockpot. In a separate bowl mix flour and water to make a paste. Add paste to soup 1 hour before serving. Serve with warm cornbread or biscuits.

-Naomi Gingerich

Navy Bean Soup

1 lb. dried navy beans
2 Tbsp. salt
Water
1 can beef or chicken broth
1 chicken bouillon cube
4 potatoes, peeled and diced

2 onions, diced
1/4 c. butter
4 carrots, sliced
2 c. ham, chopped
Salt (to taste)
Pepper (to taste)

Rinse beans and place in a large stockpot. Cover with water. Add salt and soak overnight. Drain. Bring 5 c. water, broth and bouillon cube to a boil. Reduce heat and simmer for 2 hours. Add potatoes, carrots and ham. In a separate saucepan, sauté onions in butter. Add to soup. Season with salt and pepper. Add more water if desired. Simmer until vegetables are tender. Serve with fresh bread and a green salad. Serves 8 people.

-Carol S. Miller

Yummy Chili Soup

1 lb. hamburger
1/2 tsp. minced onion
1/2 tsp. garlic
1 tsp. salt
1 Tbsp. flour
2 c. Mexican-style
kidney beans

2 Tbsp. brown sugar
2 c. tomato juice
1 small can tomato
paste
1 tsp. chili powder
(or more)

Brown hamburger. Add onion, garlic, flour, salt, brown sugar and chili powder. Add tomato juice, tomato paste and Mexican beans. Simmer for 1/2 hour. Serves 6 people.

-Jayme Shaw

Becky's Chicken Noodle Soup

3 1/2 qt. water
4 skinless, boneless
chicken breasts
6 chicken bouillon cubes
3 1/2 tsp. salt
1 tsp. pepper
1/4 tsp. cumin

1 tsp. parsley
1/8 tsp. garlic powder
1/8 tsp. thyme
2 c. carrots, chopped
1 c. celery, chopped
1 small onion, chopped
12 oz. noodles

In a saucepan, cook chicken, water and bouillon cubes for 45 minutes on medium/high heat. Remove chicken to cool. Reduce heat. Add remaining ingredients except noodles. Tear chicken apart and place back in soup. Bring to a boil. Add noodles and cook an additional 15-20 minutes or until noodles are tender. NOTE: Total cooking time is 1 1/2 hours.

-Becky Elliott

Taco Soup

1 1/2 lb. hamburger
8 oz. taco sauce
1 qt. tomatoes, diced
  or tomato juice
2 cans chili beans
1/2 c. onions, chopped

1 pkg. taco seasoning
15 oz. pizza sauce
Salt (to taste)
Pepper (to taste)

Brown hamburger and onions. Add remaining ingredients and simmer until heated through. Serve with shredded cheese, sour cream and taco chips.

-Esther Yoder

Low Fat Chicken Tortellini Soup

30 oz. low fat chicken broth
1 can cream of chicken soup
3 skinless, boneless chicken
  breast halves, diced
1 c. carrots, chopped
1 onion, chopped

2 garlic cloves, minced
1/2 tsp. oregano
1/4 tsp. basil
7 oz. cheese tortellini
10 oz. broccoli,
  frozen

Bring broth, soup, chicken, carrots, onion, garlic, oregano and basil to a boil. Add tortellini and simmer for 30 minutes. Add frozen broccoli and cook another 10 minutes or until broccoli is tender. Serves 6 people. NOTE: 1 serving: 277 calories; 23 grams protein; 31 grams carbohydrates; 6 grams fat.

-Joanne Weaver

Taco Soup

1 1/2 - 2 lb. hamburger
1 small onion
1 pkg. taco seasoning
1 qt. pizza sauce

1 qt. water
1 can chili beans or
   pork-n-beans

Brown hamburger and onion. Add taco seasoning, pizza sauce, water and beans. Simmer 15 minutes or until heated through. Serve with sour cream, shredded cheddar cheese and crumbled Doritos.

-Ruth Weaver/Carol S. Miller

Italian Zucchini Crescent Pie

4 c. zucchini, thinly sliced
1 c. onion, chopped
2 Tbsp. butter
2 Tbsp. parsley flakes
1/2 tsp. salt
1/2 tsp. pepper
1/4 tsp. garlic powder
1/4 tsp. basil leaves
1/4 tsp. oregano leaves

2 eggs, well beaten
8 oz. shredded
   Muenster cheese or
   mozzarella cheese
1 can Pillsbury
   crescent rolls
2 tsp. prepared
   mustard

In a large skillet, cook zucchini and onion in butter until tender. Stir in parsley, salt, pepper, garlic powder, basil and oregano. In a large bowl, combine eggs and cheese; mix well. Stir in cooked vegetable mixture. Separate dough into 8 triangles. Place in ungreased 10" pie pan, a 2 qt. baking dish or 11" quiche pan. Press over bottom and up sides to form crust. Firmly press perforations to seal. Spread crust with mustard. Pour egg-vegetable mixture evenly into prepared crust. Bake at 375° for approximately 20 minutes or until an inserted knife comes out clean. Let stand for 10 minutes before serving. Yield: 6 servings

-Ann Miller

84

Chinese Hoko Pot Soup

Chicken broth
Mushrooms, chopped
Green onions, chopped
Chinese noodles
Chicken, beef or ham, diced
Tofu, chopped

Chinese cabbage,
  shredded
Chinese pea pods,
  whole
Small corn cobs,
  canned and whole

Begin with 4 saucepans on the stove. Each person chooses the ingredients for their soup. Place chicken broth and meat in each pan. Cook until meat is done. Add any combination of the remaining ingredients. Cook until vegetables are crunchy, but hot. When soup is ready, dish vegetables and meat into a soup bowl. The next soup is prepared in the leftover broth by repeating the process. As each person makes their soup the flavors become more interesting because different vegetables are added. NOTE: The amount of ingredients depends on how many people you are serving and how much soup you want to make.

-Lynette Miller

Creamy Succotash

10 oz. corn, frozen
10 oz. cut green beans, frozen
10 oz. lima beans, frozen
1 large onion, finely chopped
1-2 celery stalks, chopped
10 3/4 oz. cream of celery soup

1 tsp. salt
dash of pepper
1/4 tsp. basil leaves,
  dried
3/4 c. Velveeta
  cheese, cubed

Place ingredients in a greased crockpot. Stir, mixing well. Cover and cook on high for 2 1/2 - 3 1/2 hours or on low for 6-8 hours. Serves 10-12 people.

-Wanda Schrock

Bonjan Borani

Indian Eggplant with Yogurt Sauce

1 medium onion, sliced
1/4 c. olive or vegetable oil
1 medium eggplant, cut
  into 1/2" slices
1 c. yogurt, unflavored
3 Tbsp. fresh mint, snipped
  or 1 1/2 tsp. crushed, dried mint

2 garlic cloves, finely
  chopped
1/2 tsp. salt
Dash of pepper
Paprika

In a skillet, stir onion in oil until tender. Remove onion. Cook half the eggplant over medium-high heat, turning once, until tender and golden brown (approximately 10 minutes). Repeat with remaining eggplant, adding more oil if necessary. Arrange onion and eggplant in an ungreased oblong baking dish. Mix remaining ingredients together with onion and eggplant, except paprika. Sprinkle paprika on top. Bake at 350° for 10-15 minutes or until hot and bubbly.

-Tammy Koser

Zucchini Patties

3/4 c. Bisquick mix
1/4 c. Parmesan cheese
2 eggs
2 c. zucchini, grated

1 small onion, chopped
1/2 tsp. salt
1/2 tsp. pepper
Oil or margarine

Place a thin layer of oil in a heavy skillet. Combine remaining ingredients together and drop by the tablespoon. Spread out and flatten patties as you turn them with a spatula. Fry on both sides until golden brown.

-Malinda Yoder

Zucchini Casserole

3 c. zucchini
1 c. Bisquick mix
1/2 c. onion, chopped
1/2 c. Parmesan cheese,
  grated
2 Tbsp. fresh parsley, snipped
1/2 tsp. salt
1/2 tsp. seasoned salt

1/2 c. vegetable oil
1/2 tsp. oregano, dried
1 garlic clove,
  chopped
1/2 c. Swiss cheese,
  grated
4 eggs, slightly beaten

Wash zucchini and grate with peel on. Combine ingredients together. Pour into buttered 9"x9" pan. Bake at 350° for 30 minutes. Serves 8-10 people.

-Charlene Miller

Skillet Corn In The Husk

6 ears of corn, with husks
1/2 c. butter, softened
1 tsp. Lawry's seasoned
  pepper or fresh ground pepper

String
1 Tbsp. Lawry's
  seasoned salt

Peel husks of corn back carefully, but only remove silk. In a small bowl combine butter, salt and pepper. Spread seasoned butter over each ear of corn. Smooth husks and tie ends together with a string. Arrange corn on grill over medium/hot coals. Turn every 5 minutes. Grill about 25 minutes or until tender.

-Kathy Torrence

Corn Pudding

16 oz. whole kernel corn
16 oz. cream style corn
1 c. sour cream
1 stick butter, melted

1 egg, beaten
1 pkg. Jiffy corn
  muffin mix

Mix ingredients together. Pour into a 2 qt. baking dish and cover. Bake at 350° for 45 minutes. Uncover and bake 15 minutes longer, until top is golden brown. Serves 6 people.

-Erma Yoder/Kathy Marner/Ruth Weaver

Corn Fairfax

1 stick butter
1/4 c. onion, minced
1/4 c. celery, chopped
1 tsp. salt
2 Tbsp. flour
1/4 c. milk
1 small pkg. frozen French
  cut green beans

1 small can cream
  style corn
2 eggs, beaten
1 Tbsp. fresh parsley,
  chopped

TOPPING:
2/3 c. fine bread crumbs
1/3 c. cheddar cheese, grated

1/2 stick butter,
  melted

Sauté onion and celery in butter. Stir in salt, flour and milk then add corn. Steam green beans and add to corn mixture. Add eggs and parsley. Place mixture into a buttered baking dish. Combine topping ingredients. Cover corn mixture with topping. Bake at 325° for 20 minutes. Serves 4-6 people.

-Charlene Miller

88

Zucchini Squares

1/2 c. onions, chopped
1/2 c. vegetable oil
3 c. zucchini, grated
3 eggs
1 c. Bisquick mix

1/2 c. Parmesan
  cheese, grated
2 tsp. parsley
1/2 tsp. oregano
1/2 tsp. garlic powder

Sauté onions in oil. In a mixing bowl combine remaining ingredients together. Add onions and pour into a 9"x13" pan. Bake at 350° for 30 minutes. Cut into squares and serve. Serves 6-8 people.

-Alma Spires

Scalloped Cauliflower

1 large head of cauliflower
3 hard-boiled eggs, diced
1 tsp. salt water

1 c. bread crumbs,
  buttered
1/4 c. cheese, grated

MEDIUM WHITE SAUCE:
4 Tbsp. butter
4 Tbsp. flour
1/4 tsp. pepper

1 tsp. salt
2 c. milk
1/2 tsp. salt

Prepare medium white sauce by melting butter in a saucepan or in the top of a double boiler. Add flour, 1/2 tsp. salt and pepper. Stir until well blended. Slowly add milk, stirring constantly, until smooth paste is formed. Break the head of cauliflower into flowerets and cook in salt water, using 1 tsp. salt, until tender. Drain. Alternate layers of cauliflower, diced eggs and white sauce in a greased baking dish. End with a layer of buttered crumbs and grated cheese on the top. Bake at 375° for 25 minutes. Serves 6 people.

-Alma Spires

Honey-Glazed Carrots

10-12 young, small carrots
(approximately 1 1/4 lb.)
3 Tbsp. butter

2 Tbsp. honey
1 Tbsp. brown sugar
Salt water

Place a small amount of salt water in a large skillet. Bring water to a boil. Add carrots, cover and cook for 8-10 minutes or until tender. Drain carrots and remove from skillet. To make the glaze, melt butter in the same skillet. Stir in honey and brown sugar. Cook and stir over medium heat about 2 minutes or until slightly thickened and bubbly. Add carrots, tossing gently with glaze until coated and heated through. Serves 4-6 people.

-Gloria Gerber

Amish Dressing

1 loaf bread
6 eggs, well beaten
2 c. milk
1/2 c. carrots, shredded
1 c. celery, finely chopped
1 c. potatoes, cubed and boiled
1 pt. chicken bits and broth

Parsley
1/4 c. onion, finely
chopped
2 tsp. chicken soup
base
Salt (to taste)
Pepper (to taste)

Cube bread and toast in butter in a frying pan. Add remaining ingredients. Fry in butter until lightly browned. Transfer to a baking dish and bake at 325° for 45 minutes.

-Elsie Schrock

Baked Sweet Potatoes

3 c. sweet potatoes,
  cooked and mashed
2 eggs, beaten
1/2 c. sugar
1/2 tsp. salt

1/4 c. margarine,
  melted
1/2 c. milk
1/2 tsp. vanilla

TOPPING:
1/2 c. brown sugar
1/3 c. flour
1/3 c. margarine, melted

1 c. pecans, chopped

Mix sweet potatoes, eggs, sugar, salt, margarine, milk and vanilla together. Place in 1 1/2 qt. casserole dish. Mix topping ingredients together. Place on top of sweet potato mixture. Bake at 350° for 35 minutes. Serves 4-6 people.

-Sharon Gerber

Sweet Potato Pancakes

1/4 c. all-purpose flour
1/2 tsp. dried rosemary
  leaves, crushed
1/8 tsp. ground black pepper
3 c. raw sweet potatoes, shredded

1 c. Egg Beaters
1/3 c. onion, chopped
1 Tbsp. margarine
Fat free sour cream

In a small bowl, combine flour, rosemary and pepper. Set aside. In a medium bowl combine sweet potatoes, Egg Beaters and onion. Stir in flour mixture. In a large nonstick skillet melt 2 tsp. margarine for each pancake. Spoon 1/3 c. potato mixture into skillet, spreading into a 4" circle. Cook for 5 minutes on each side. Remove and keep warm. Serve hot with sour cream. Serves 8 people. NOTE: 1 serving=127 calories.

-Joanne Weaver

Baked Sweet Potato Slices

6 sweet potatoes
1 c. brown sugar
1/4 c. butter

1/4 c. water
1/2 tsp. salt

Boil sweet potatoes until tender. Cool. Peel each potato and slice into 4 slices, 2" thick. Place sweet potatoes in a baking dish. In a saucepan boil brown sugar, butter, water and salt. Pour over potatoes and bake at 350° for 30 minutes. Yield: 6 servings

-Chris Bower

Parmesan Potatoes

6 large potatoes, peeled and
  quartered, sliced in rounds
  or as French fries
1/4 c. flour
1/4 c. Parmesan cheese, grated

3/4 tsp. salt
1/8 tsp. pepper
1/3 c. margarine
  or butter
Water

Combine flour, cheese, salt and pepper in a bag. Moisten potatoes with water. Shake a few potatoes at a time in the bag. Coat well with cheese. Melt butter in a 9"x13" baking pan or a cookie sheet with sides. Place potatoes in a single layer in the pan. Bake at 350-375° for 1 hour, turning halfway through. Serves 6 people.

-Alma Spires/Jayme Shaw

Potatoes Au Gratin

26 oz. hash brown potatoes,
  frozen and shredded
2 c. Half and Half
1/4 c. + 1 Tbsp. butter
1/2 tsp. salt
1/2 c. Parmesan cheese

8-10 slices Velveeta
  cheese
1/4 tsp. garlic salt
  (optional)

*Rub 1 Tbsp. of butter over the bottom of a 9"x13" baking pan.
Sprinkle with garlic salt. Pour potatoes into the pan. Sprinkle
salt and Parmesan cheese over potatoes. Heat the Half and
Half with 1/4 c. butter and pour over potatoes. Cover with
Velveeta cheese. Bake uncovered at 375° for 50 minutes.
Serves 6 people.*

-Naomi Gingerich

Cheesy Potatoes

2 lbs. hash brown
  potatoes, frozen
2 small cans cream
  of celery soup
1 Tbsp. onion powder
1/2 c. butter, melted

Salt (to taste)
Pepper (to taste)
1/2 c. onion, chopped
1 c. sour cream
2 c. cheddar cheese
Cornflakes, crushed

*Mix ingredients together, except cornflakes and enough
cheese to cover the top. Place mixture in a 9"x13" baking dish.
Place remaining cheese on top and put cornflakes on top of
that. Bake at 350° for 1 hour. Serves 4 people.*

-Beth Ernst

Potluck Potatoes

2 lbs. hash brown
  potatoes, frozen
1/2 c. butter, melted
1 tsp. salt
1/2 tsp. pepper
1/2 c. onion, chopped

1 can cream of
  chicken soup
1 pt. sour cream
2 c. Velveeta cheese,
  cubed

TOPPING:
2 c. cornflakes, crushed   1/4 c. melted butter

In a large bowl, combine potatoes with butter. Heat soup, onion, salt, pepper, sour cream and cheese until cheese is melted. Pour over potatoes and mix thoroughly. Pour into a greased baking dish. Combine topping ingredients. Place on top of potatoes. Cover and bake at 350° for 45 minutes. Serves 8 people.

-Naomi Gingerich

Spinach Mashed Potatoes

6-8 large potatoes, peeled,
  cooked and mashed
1 c. sour cream
2 tsp. salt
1/4 tsp. pepper
2 Tbsp. chives, chopped
  or green onion tops

1/4 c. butter or
  margarine
10 oz. pkg. spinach,
  chopped, thawed
  and well drained
1 c. cheddar cheese,
  shredded

In a large bowl, combine ingredients together except cheese. Spoon into a greased 2 qt. casserole dish. Bake uncovered at 400° for 15 minutes. Top with cheese and bake 5 minutes longer. Yield: 6-8 servings

-Ann Miller

Hot German Potato Salad

6 c. potatoes, diced
9 slices bacon, diced
1/3 c. vinegar
3 Tbsp. sugar
1 1/2 Tbsp. prepared mustard
1 Tbsp. parsley, chopped
1/2 c. onions, finely chopped
3 Tbsp. bacon drippings
2 Tbsp. all-purpose flour
1 1/3 c. water
3 hard-boiled eggs, sliced
1 tsp. salt
1/8 tsp. pepper
Salt water

In a saucepan, cook potatoes in boiling salt water until tender. Drain potatoes; keep warm. Cook bacon until crisp; crumble and set aside. Drain all but 3 Tbsp. of drippings. Sauté onions in drippings until tender. Stir in flour, salt and pepper; blend well. Add sugar, water and vinegar. Boil for 2 minutes. Pour over potatoes. Stir gently to coat. Add bacon, mustard, parsley and eggs; mix thoroughly. Serve warm.

-Elsie Schrock

"Faith that something can be done
is the essential ingredient to any achievement."
-Thomas N. Carruther-

"Laughter is brightest
when food is best."

-Irish Proverb-

Meats,
Main Dishes,
& Sauces

Chicken Cordon Bleu

Skinless, boneless
  chicken breasts
Muenster cheese or
  Farmer's cheese
Virginia baked ham
Egg wash (eggs mixed with some milk)

Cornflake crumbs
  mixed with some
  Parmesan cheese
  and Italian bread
  crumbs

Place Saran Wrap over chicken and beat with tenderizer until each piece is approximately 1/2" thick. Place 1 slice of ham on chicken. Place 1 slice of cheese on ham. Roll up. Roll in egg mixture. Coat in crumb coating. Place in 9"x13" pan. Use toothpicks to hold chicken together. Bake at 350° for approximately 45 minutes or until done. Remove toothpicks before serving. NOTE: Use 1 piece of chicken, cheese and ham per person.

-Mandy Beachy

Bacon Wrapped Chicken

6 skinless, boneless chicken
  breasts, halved
1 carton cream cheese with
  onion and chives, softened

1 Tbsp. butter
Salt (to taste)
6 bacon strips

Place Saran Wrap over chicken and beat with tenderizer until each piece is approximately 1/2" thick. Spread 3 Tbsp. cream cheese over each piece. Dot with butter and sprinkle with salt. Wrap each piece with a bacon strip. Place seam down in a greased 9"x13" baking pan. Bake uncovered at 400° for 35 minutes or until bacon is clear. Broil 6" from the heat for 5 minutes or until bacon is crisp. Serves 8 people.

-Carol S. Miller

Chicken Divan

3 skinless chicken breasts, chopped and cooked
2 pkg. broccoli, frozen (optional)
21 1/2 oz. cream of chicken soup
1 c. Hellman's mayonnaise (not salad dressing)
8 oz. sour cream
Rice

1 Tbsp. lemon juice
1 tsp. curry powder
1 c. sharp cheddar cheese, shredded
1/3 c. Parmesan cheese, shredded
Paprika (for color)
Salt (to taste)
Pepper (to taste)

Cook broccoli and drain. Place broccoli (or chicken if not using broccoli), on the bottom of a greased 9"x13" baking pan. Sprinkle Parmesan cheese over broccoli or chicken. Place chicken on top of broccoli and Parmesan cheese. Sprinkle half of the cheddar cheese on top. Mix soup, mayonnaise, sour cream, lemon juice, salt, pepper and curry powder together. Pour over chicken and cheese. Sprinkle remaining cheddar cheese over sauce. Sprinkle with paprika. Bake at 350° for 30-40 minutes. Serve over rice. Serves 4-6 people.

-John Gross

Chicken Breasts

4 slices bacon
4 boneless chicken breasts
4 oz. beef, dried

1/2 pt. sour cream
1 can cream of mushroom soup

Wrap 1 slice of bacon around each chicken breast. Place chicken on a slice of beef. Mix sour cream and mushroom soup together. Pour over meat. Place in a single layer in an 8"x12" pan. Do not salt. Bake uncovered at 275° for 3 hours.

-Sara Mae Stutzman

Chicken Breasts

8 boneless, skinless chicken breasts
1/2 - 3/4 lb. Swiss cheese, sliced
2 cans cream of mushroom soup
1/2 c. sour cream
1/4 c. white cooking sherry
2 c. Pepperidge Farm herb stuffing mix
1/2 c. margarine or butter, melted

Place chicken in a 9"x13" baking dish. Cover chicken with Swiss cheese. In a bowl, combine soup, sour cream and cooking sherry. Pour over cheese. In a separate bowl, combine butter and stuffing mix. Sprinkle over top of the soup mixture. Bake at 325° for 1 - 1 1/4 hours.

-Heidi Smith

Chicken Parmigiana

4 boneless, skinless chicken breasts, halved
6 oz. tomato paste
3/4 c. water
2 garlic cloves, minced or 1/4 tsp. garlic salt
1 Tbsp. parsley flakes
1 tsp. salt
1/4 tsp. pepper
1/2 tsp. Italian seasonings
1/2 tsp. oregano
1/4 tsp. red pepper flakes, crushed
16 oz. mozzarella cheese, shredded
1/4 c. Parmesan cheese, grated

Place chicken in a greased 8" square baking pan. In a saucepan, combine tomato paste, water, garlic, parsley, salt, pepper, Italian seasonings, oregano and red pepper. Bring to a boil. Pour over chicken. Bake uncovered at 400° for 15-20 minutes or until chicken juices run clear. Sprinkle with cheeses. Bake for 10 more minutes or until cheese is melted. Serves 4 people.

-Kristi Gross

Italian Garden Chicken

8 oz. wide noodles
6-8 c. chicken broth
1 lb. boneless, skinless
  chicken breasts, halved
1/4 c. Ranch dressing
1/3 c. Italian-style dry
  bread crumbs
2 Tbsp. olive or
  vegetable oil
4-6 Roma tomatoes,
  cut in large pieces
1 large onion,
  cut in large strips

2 c. fresh mushrooms,
  halved or quartered
4 Tbsp. salted butter
1 Tbsp. Italian
  seasoning
Parmesan cheese,
  grated
Parsley, chopped
Salt (to taste)
Pepper (to taste)

*Coat chicken with Ranch dressing and dip into bread crumbs.
Cook noodles in chicken broth. In a skillet, heat oil on medium-high heat. Cook chicken in oil for 12-15 minutes, turning
once. While chicken is cooking, heat another skillet to medium-high heat. Cook onions and mushrooms in butter until
soft. Add tomatoes and cook just until heated through.
Sprinkle vegetables with Italian seasoning, salt and pepper. To
serve, layer on individual plates beginning with noodles, then
chicken, then vegetables. Sprinkle with Parmesan cheese and
parsley. Serves 4 people.*

-Vicki Yoder

Crispy Baked Chicken

1/2 c. cornmeal
1 1/2 tsp. salt
1/2 tsp. dried oregano
1/2 c. all-purpose flour
1 1/2 tsp. chili powder

1/4 tsp. pepper
1 broiler/fryer chicken,
  cut up
1/2 c. milk
1/3 c. butter, melted

Combine cornmeal, salt, oregano, flour, chili powder and pepper. Dip chicken in milk. Roll in cornmeal mixture. Place in a greased 9"x13" pan. Drizzle with butter. Bake uncovered at 375° for 55 minutes.

-Christina Troyer

Picnic Chicken

4 boneless, skinless chicken
  breasts, halved
1 c. dry bread crumbs
1/2 tsp. dried parsley flakes
1/2 tsp. garlic salt
1/4 tsp. pepper

1/4 tsp. paprika
1/8 tsp. dried thyme
1 egg, lightly beaten
1 Tbsp. cooking oil
1 Tbsp. butter or
  margarine

*Pound chicken to 1/4" thick. In a shallow bowl, combine crumbs, parsley, garlic salt, pepper, paprika and thyme. Dip chicken in egg. Roll chicken in crumb mixture. In a medium skillet, brown chicken in oil and butter over medium heat for 3-5 minutes on each side or until juices run clear.
Serves 4 people.*

-Kristi Gross

Sour Cream Chicken

1 c. Pepperidge Farm
  herb stuffing
1/2 c. Parmesan cheese
2 Tbsp. parsley

1/2 c. butter, melted
1 c. sour cream
3 lb. chicken, skinless

Wash and dry chicken. Combine stuffing, cheese, parsley and butter together. Coat chicken with sour cream. Roll in crumbs. Place on a cookie sheet so they are not touching. Bake at 375° for 45-55 minutes, until tender. It is not necessary to turn.

-Marjorie Weiss

Chicken Fingers

Boneless, skinless chicken
  breasts, cut in strips
2 c. crackers, crushed fine
3/4 c. Parmesan cheese
2 Tbsp. parsley

1 tsp. pepper
1/2 tsp. garlic salt
1 1/2 tsp. salt
1 c. butter, melted

Mix crackers, cheese, garlic salt, parsley, salt and pepper together in a plastic bag. Shake well. Dip chicken strips in melted butter, then drop in plastic bag. Shake enough to coat. (Only do a few strips in the bag at a time.) Arrange coated strips in a shallow baking dish. Bake uncovered at 350° for 1 hour or until tender.

-Naomi Gingerich

Bow Tie Chicken

8 oz. bow tie pasta, cooked
1 1/2 lb. or 4 boneless
  chicken breasts
1/2 lb. peppered bacon
1 c. onions, sliced
1 c. mushrooms, sliced
3 Tbsp. olive oil
1 Tbsp. garlic, minced
1/2 tsp. pepper
Salt (to taste)

1/4 tsp. onion powder
2 Tbsp. flour
14 oz. chicken broth
6 oz. baby spinach,
  fresh
6 oz. corn, frozen
16 oz. sour cream
1/2 c. green onion,
  chopped
5 oz. croutons, crushed

Fry bacon until completely cooked. Drain, reserving 1 Tbsp. of bacon drippings. Add onions, mushrooms and garlic. Continue to saute until everything is cooked, approximately 5 minutes. Remove mixture and set aside. Cut chicken into 1" pieces. Sprinkle with flour, onion powder, salt and pepper. Sauté in oil until lightly browned. Add chicken broth and mushroom mixture to pan. Cover and simmer 10 minutes. Stir in sour cream until completely blended. Add corn and spinach. Stir. Cover and simmer for 2 minutes. Mix with pasta. Sprinkle with croutons and onions. Serve immediately. Serves 6-8 people.

-Mabel Campbell

Honey Baked Chicken

3 lb. chicken, chopped
1/3 c. butter, melted
1/3 c. honey

2 Tbsp. mustard
1 tsp. salt
1 tsp. curry powder

Arrange chicken in a shallow pan. Combine butter, honey, mustard, salt and curry powder together. Pour over chicken. Bake 1 hour and 15 minutes, basting every 15 minutes, until chicken is tender and brown. NOTE: Really good served with rice. Serves 4-6 people.

-Wanda Schrock

Chicken Broccoli Casserole

3 c. broccoli, cooked
  until tender
2 c. chicken, cooked and cubed
1 can cream of chicken soup
1/2 c. Miracle Whip

1/2 c. Parmesan
  cheese
1/2 tsp. curry powder
1 c. fresh bread, cubed
2 Tbsp. butter, melted

Place broccoli in a greased 9"x13" pan. Combine chicken, soup, Miracle Whip, cheese and curry powder together in a bowl. Spoon over broccoli. Combine butter and bread crumbs. Sprinkle over top. Bake at 350° for 30 minutes. Serves 4 people.

-Pam Buss

Crockpot Chicken, Broccoli and Rice

16 oz. broccoli, frozen
2 cans cream of
  mushroom soup
1 stick margarine
2 soup cans of water

1 onion, chopped
16 oz. Velveeta
  cheese, cubed
2 1/2 c. minute rice
1 lb. can cooked
  chicken

Cook broccoli until soft. Add soup, margarine, water, onion and Velveeta cheese. Simmer on low until cheese is melted. Stir in rice and chicken. Place in crockpot. Cook on high for 2 hours. NOTE: This can be made the night before and refrigerated. Cook on high for 3 hours. Serves 6 people.

-Sharon Gerber

Chicken Casserole

6 c. bread
1/4 c. butter
1 Tbsp. onion, chopped
1 Tbsp. parsley flakes
1/4 c. butter, melted
1 c. chicken broth
4 Tbsp. flour

1 can cream of
  chicken soup
1 soup can of milk
2 eggs
2 c. chicken, cooked
Seasonings of your
  choice (to taste)

Combine unmelted butter, onion and parsley and spread on bread. Toast in a pan; set aside. In a saucepan, combine melted butter, chicken broth, flour, soup and milk. Cook until paste consistency. Add eggs, chicken and seasonings. Pour chicken over top of bread. Bake at 300° for 1 1/2 hours. Serves 7-8 people.

-Katie Obbliger

Chicken Casserole

6-10 boneless, skinless
  chicken breasts, halved
1 lb. bacon
1 pkg. chipped dried
  beef, chopped
1 can cream of
  mushroom soup

1 pt. sour cream
1/8 tsp. cayenne red
  pepper
2 Tbsp. vinegar
1 Tbsp. sugar
1 Tbsp. lemon juice
Rice, cooked

Place beef pieces in a 3 qt. baking dish. Wrap each piece of chicken with a piece of bacon. Lay chicken side by side on top of beef. Mix mushroom soup, sour cream, red pepper, vinegar, sugar and lemon juice together. Pour over chicken pieces. Bake at 275° for 2 1/2 - 3 hours. Serve chicken and sauce over rice. NOTE: You can double the sauce mixture, to make sure there is plenty to serve over the rice.

-Sharon Gerber

Festive Chicken Fajitas

1/2 c. olive oil
1/2 c. lime juice
  (approximately 3 juicy limes)
2 cloves garlic, minced
1 tsp. salt
1 tsp. pepper
1 tsp. sugar
1 tsp. oregano
Onions, diced
Tomatoes

Sour cream
Salsa
1 tsp. ground cumin
3 whole skinless,
  boneless chicken
  breasts, flattened
12 flour tortillas,
  wrapped in
  aluminum foil

Combine olive oil, lime juice, garlic, salt, pepper, sugar, oregano and cumin in a sealable plastic bag. Add chicken and seal. Turn to coat. Marinate 8 hours. Turn your grill on to heat the coals. When they are hot, place drained chicken and foil-wrapped tortillas on grill. Cook for 3-4 minutes per side. Remove tortillas and chicken. Slice chicken in 1/2" strips. Serve chicken on tortillas with onions, tomatoes, sour cream and salsa. Serves 6 people.

-Tara Lynn Smith

Taco Meatloaf

1 c. crackers, crushed
1 envelope taco mix
1/2 c. ketchup
1 can mushrooms,
  drained
1 can sliced olives,
  drained

1 small onion, chopped
2 eggs, beaten
2 Tbsp. Worcestershire
  sauce
2 lb. lean ground beef

In a bowl combine all ingredients together except beef. Mix well; add beef and mix again. Press into a greased 9"x13" pan. Bake uncovered at 350° for 1 hour. Serve with sour cream, salsa and cheddar cheese. Serves 8 people.

-Carol S. Miller

Citrus Chicken Stir Fry

1 lb. skinless, boneless
  chicken breasts
1 Tbsp. cooking oil
1 lb. stir fry vegetables
1/2 c. stir fry sauce

1/2 c. orange juice
2 Tbsp. brown sugar
2 c. rice, cooked and
  hot
1/4 c. almonds, sliced

Cook chicken and cut into strips. In a large skillet, heat oil to medium-high and add vegetables. Stir fry for 5 minutes. Add stir fry sauce, orange juice and brown sugar. Continue cooking over medium heat for 3 minutes. Toss chicken with vegetable mixture. Serve over rice and top with almonds.

-Kathy Torrence

Chicken Curry
Authentic Indian Recipe

1 1/2-2 lb. chicken
  breasts, cubed
5 Tbsp. oil
1 medium onion, minced
4 cloves garlic, minced
1/2" piece ginger, minced
8 oz. can tomato sauce
1 small can tomato paste
1 tsp. cardamom

4 cloves
1 tsp. cinnamon
1/4 tsp. turmeric
  powder
1 tsp. ground cumin
1 tsp. nutmeg
Salt (to taste)
Lime juice (to taste)
Handful of cilantro
  leaves, chopped

Heat oil. Fry onion, ginger and garlic until soft. Add cardamom, cloves, cinnamon, turmeric, cumin, nutmeg and salt. Fry briefly. Add chicken and fry until golden brown. Add tomato sauce and tomato paste. Cover tightly and cook until chicken is done. Sprinkle with lime juice and cilantro leaves. Serve hot over hot white rice.

-Vicki Yoder

India's Tandoori Murghi

Roast Chicken with Spiced Yogurt

3-4 lb. broiler/fryer
  chicken, chopped
1/4 tsp. and 1/4 c. water
1/4 tsp. dry mustard
1 c. unflavored yogurt
1/4 c. lemon juice
1 clove garlic, chopped

1/2 tsp. cardamom
1/4 tsp. ground ginger
1/4 tsp. ground cumin
1/4 tsp. crushed
  red peppers
1/4 tsp. pepper
1 1/2 tsp. salt

Place chicken in a bowl. Mix 1/4 tsp. water and mustard in a separate bowl (1 qt.). Stir in yogurt, lemon juice, garlic, salt, cardamom, ginger, cumin, red peppers and pepper. Pour over chicken; turn to coat well. Cover and marinate in refrigerator for 12-24 hours. Place chicken on a rack in a shallow roasting pan, reserving marinade. Roast uncovered at 375° for 1 hour and 45 minutes-2 hours and 15 minutes or until thickest pieces are done. Baste with reserved marinade during last 30 minutes of roasting and cover with a loose tent of aluminum foil. Remove chicken from pan; stir 1/4 c. water into marinade. Heat just until hot. Serve with chicken.

-Tammy Koser

Nepali Chicken Curry

2 lb. broiler chicken,
  chopped into small pieces
1 c. onion, diced
4 cloves garlic
1 tsp. turmeric
Coriander
1 tsp. ground cumin
1/2 tsp. ground ginger
1 tsp. chili powder or
  paprika (optional)
2 bay leaves
1 c. tomatoes,
  chopped
1 tsp. curry powder
Oil
Water

Fry onion in oil until golden brown. Mix garlic, turmeric, cumin, coriander, ginger and chili powder with some water to make a paste. Add paste to onions and fry for 3-4 minutes. Stir in bay leaves and tomatoes. Add chicken and mix thoroughly. Cover and heat slowly until meat becomes tender, approximately 15 minutes. Add curry powder and cook for 2-3 minutes longer. Cover until ready to serve. Serve hot over rice. NOTE: Hot water can be added if contents dry up while cooking. For variation you can substitute 1/2 c. yogurt for the tomatoes.

-Gopal and Sheila Sharma (Nepal)

Curry Rice Dish

1 1/4 c. brown rice, cooked
1 c. celery, chopped
1 small onion, chopped
1 can water chestnuts, sliced
1 can mushrooms (or fresh)
1 c. Hellman's mayonnaise
1 tsp. curry powder
Salt (to taste)
Pepper (to taste)
Approximately 2 lb.
  chicken, crab, tuna
  or shrimp, cooked
1 tsp. Worcestershire
  or soy sauce

Mix ingredients together in a casserole dish. Bake at 350° for 45 minutes. Serves 12 people.

-Marilyn Hartman

Balti Chicken Madras (India)

1 Tbsp. oil
1 onion, chopped
1 lb. boneless chicken
  breast, cubed

4 potatoes, peeled
  and diced

SAUCE:
1 tsp. chili powder
1/2 tsp. ground ginger
1 1/2 tsp. ground coriander
1 tsp. minced garlic
1/4 tsp. turmeric

1 Tbsp. curry powder
2 Tbsp. lemon juice
8 oz. tomato sauce
1 tsp. salt
3/4 c. water

Mix sauce ingredients together. Set aside. Heat oil in frying pan and fry onions until golden brown. Add chicken and stir fry 1 minute. Add potatoes and sauce. Bring to a boil; cover and simmer for 15 minutes. Serve over rice. Serves 4 people.

-Angie Peck

Chicken Curry (Nepal)

2 Tbsp. oil
2 1/2 - 3 lb. broiler
  chicken, chopped
1 tsp. salt
1 medium onion, chopped

2 Tbsp. water
1 c. sour cream
2 tsp. curry powder
1/8 tsp. ground ginger
1/8 tsp. ground cumin

Heat oil in a skillet until hot. Cook chicken over medium heat until brown on all sides, approximately 15 minutes. Drain fat. Sprinkle chicken with salt, onion and water. Cook and simmer until thickest pieces are done. Remove chicken from skillet; keep warm. Pour liquid from skillet into a bowl; skim fat. Remove 1/4 c. liquid to skillet. Stir in sour cream, curry powder, ginger and cumin. Heat, stirring constantly, just until hot. Pour sauce over chicken. Serve with rice and Mango Chutney.

-Tammy Koser

South India Curry

2 potatoes, quartered
1 can peas
1/4 lb. butter or margarine
1 onion, chopped
1 small green pepper,
  chopped
2 tsp. curry powder
1 c. cauliflower, chopped

1 small can mushrooms
1/4 c. cashews
1 c. tomato sauce
1 tsp. sugar
1 Tbsp. lemon juice
Salt (to taste)
1 c. water (as needed)

Sauté onions, peppers and curry powder in butter and stir. Add potatoes and peas. Cook 10 minutes. Add cauliflower, mushrooms and cashews. Stir in tomato sauce with water. Add sugar and simmer until done but not mushy. Add salt and lemon juice. Serve over cooked rice.

-Marva Peck

Sweet & Sour Chicken

2 - 3 1/2 lb. broiler
  chicken, chopped
20 oz. pineapple slices
  in heavy syrup

8 oz. creamy French
  salad dressing
1 envelope onion
  - soup mix

Prepare approximately 1 1/2 hours before serving. In a large roasting pan, arrange chicken, skin side up, in 1 layer. Drain pineapple syrup into a medium bowl. Stir in French dressing and onion mix. Pour sauce over chicken. Bake at 375° for 1 hour, basting occasionally. Cut each pineapple slice in half. Add pineapples to roasting pan, turning to coat with sauce mixture. Bake 15 minutes longer or until chicken is tender. To serve, arrange chicken and pineapple on warm large platter. Skim fat from sauce in pan. Pour sauce over chicken. Serves 8 people.

-Sara Mae Stutzman

Cashew Chicken (India)

2 medium onions
3/4 c. cashew nuts
8 oz. tomato sauce
1 Tbsp. curry powder
2 tsp. minced garlic
1 1/2 tsp. chili powder
2 Tbsp. lemon juice
1/2 tsp. turmeric
1/2 c. water

1 tsp. salt
1 c. plain lowfat yogurt
1 Tbsp. oil
2 Tbsp. fresh coriander,
chopped (optional)
1 lb. chicken breasts,
cubed
2 c. mushrooms, fresh

Place onions and 1/2 c. cashew nuts in food processor and process for 1 minute. Add tomato sauce, curry powder, garlic, chili power, lemon juice, turmeric, salt and yogurt. Process 1 or 2 minutes. In a saucepan heat oil over medium heat. Add spice mixture. Fry for 2 minutes. Add half the coriander, if available, and chicken. Fry for 1 minute. Add mushrooms and water. Cover and simmer for 15 minutes. Garnish with remaining coriander and cashew nuts. Serve over rice. Serves 4 people.

-Angie Peck

Baked Chicken Salad

2 large boiled chicken
breasts, cubed
1 c. celery, diced
10 oz. cream of
chicken soup
1 Tbsp. onion,
finely chopped
8 oz. water chestnuts, chopped

1/2 tsp. salt
1/2 tsp. pepper
1 Tbsp. lemon juice
1/2 c. mayonnaise
3 hard-boiled eggs
2 c. potato chips,
crushed

Mix all ingredients together thoroughly, except potato chips. Place in a baking dish. Cover with potato chips. Bake at 350° for 1/2 hour. Serves 4-6 people.

-Diana Henry

Turkey Rice Casserole

1 c. long grain rice, uncooked
1/2 c. onion, chopped
1/4 c. butter or margarine, melted
2 1/4 c. chicken broth
1/2 c. green pepper, chopped

1 1/2 c. chicken, turkey or ham, cubed
3 oz. sliced mushrooms, drained
Shredded cheddar or American cheese
1/2 c. celery, diced

In a skillet brown rice and onion in butter over medium heat, stirring occasionally. Add chicken broth; cover and cook 10 minutes. Add green pepper and celery. Cook covered for 10-15 minutes longer, or until rice is tender, stirring occasionally. Add meat and mushrooms; mix well. Transfer to a 1 1/2 qt. baking dish. Bake covered at 350° for 15-20 minutes. Remove casserole from oven. Sprinkle with desired amount of cheese. Return to oven until cheese is melted. Serves 5-6 people.

-Heidi Hershberger

Hot Chicken Salad

2 c. chicken, chopped &
  cooked
1 c. celery, chopped
1/2 c. almonds, toasted
1/2 tsp. salt
1/4 tsp. tarragon
2 tsp. onion, dried or chopped

2 Tbsp. lemon juice
1 can water chest-
  nuts, chopped
1 c. Hellman's
  mayonnaise

Toast almonds on low temperature in a non-stick pan for 10-15 minutes. Mix chicken, celery, almonds and salt. In a separate bowl mix remaining ingredients and add to chicken mixture. Place in casserole and bake at 450° for 15-20 minutes. NOTE: Three 5 oz. cans of chicken can be used in place of 2 c. chicken.

-Ann Miller

Hot Chicken Salad

2 1/2 c. chicken,
  diced and cooked
1 1/2 c. celery, diced
1 c. bread, cubed
1/2 c. almonds (optional)
1/2 tsp. salt

1 c. mayonnaise
2 Tbsp. lemon juice
1 c. cheese, grated
1 c. potato chips,
  crumbled

Mix chicken, celery, bread, almonds and salt together. Place in a 9"x13" baking dish. Stir lemon juice and mayonnaise together. Spread on top of chicken like icing. Sprinkle cheese and chips on top. Bake at 450° for 15 minutes or until cheese melts.

-Joyce Weaver

Salisbury Steak

MEAT INGREDIENTS:

2 lb. hamburger
2 eggs
2 c. cracker crumbs
1/2 c. ketchup

2 tsp. salt
2 Tbsp. minced onion
1/2 tsp. pepper
1 tsp. Worcestershire
  sauce

SAUCE:

1 can cream of
  mushroom soup
2 Tbsp. butter

1/2 tsp. garlic salt
1 c. milk

Mix meat ingredients together. Press into a cookie sheet and refrigerate at least 2 hours. Cut into squares. Roll in flour and fry in pan, browning both sides. Place into a baking dish. Mix sauce ingredients together. Cover with sauce. Bake covered at 350° for 1 hour.

-Geneva Schlabach

Naomi's Pot Roast

3 lb. roast
1 large onion,
  chopped
1/2 green pepper,
  chopped
1 1/2 c. ketchup
1 tsp. salt

1/2 tsp. pepper
1 tsp. Worcestershire
  sauce
1/2 tsp. mustard
1/2 tsp. red pepper,
  chopped (optional)

Mix all ingredients together. Pour over roast. Bake covered at 300°-325° for 4 hours until very tender, turning roast occasionally. If mixture gets too thick while cooking, add a small amount of water. Serves 6-8 people.

-Naomi Gingerich

Barbecued Meatballs

Meatballs:

1 1/2 lb. hamburger
1 c. quick oats
1/2 c. onion, chopped
1 tsp. pepper

2/3 c. evaporated milk
1 egg
1/4 tsp. garlic powder
1 tsp. chili powder

SAUCE:

1 c. ketchup
1/4 c. onion, chopped
1 tsp. liquid smoke

3/4 c. brown sugar
1/4 tsp. garlic powder

To make meatballs mix all meatball ingredients well and roll in balls about the size of large walnuts. Mix sauce ingredients together, stirring until brown sugar is dissolved. Pour over meatballs before baking. Bake at 350° for 45-50 minutes. Makes 30 meatballs. NOTE: Meatballs can be made ahead and frozen.

-Wanda Schrock

Bul-Ko-Kee

Korean Barbecued Beef

1 lb. beef, boneless
   top sirloin, etc.
1/4 c. soy sauce
3 Tbsp. sugar
2 Tbsp. sesame or
   vegetable oil

1/4 tsp. pepper
3 green onions,
   finely chopped
2 cloves garlic,
   chopped

Trim fat from beef; cut beef diagonally across grain into 1/8" slices. Mix remaining ingredients together; stir in beef until well coated. Cover and refrigerate 30 minutes. Drain beef; stir fry in skillet or wok over medium heat until light brown, 2-3 minutes. Add vegetables if desired. Serve beef over hot cooked rice.

-Tammy Koser

Barbecued Meatballs

MEAT MIXTURE:

3 lb. ground beef
12 oz. evaporated milk
1 c. oatmeal
1 c. cracker crumbs
2 eggs

1/2 c. onion, chopped
1/2 tsp. garlic powder
2 tsp. chili powder
2 tsp. salt
1/2 tsp. pepper

SAUCE:

2 c. ketchup
1 c. brown sugar
1 Tbsp. Worcestershire sauce
  or 1/2 tsp. liquid smoke

1/2 tsp. garlic powder
1/4 c. onions,
  chopped

Combine meat mixture ingredients together; mixture will be soft. Form into walnut size balls and place in a baking dish. Mix sauce ingredients and pour over top of meatballs. Cover and bake at 350° for 1 hour. NOTE: Meatballs can be placed on a cookie sheet and browned in the oven at 400° for 10 minutes before putting them in a baking casserole and covering with sauce. They may also be made ahead and frozen. Line cookie sheet with wax paper and place meatballs in a single layer on cookie sheet. Place in freezer until frozen solid; store in freezer bags. Allow increased baking time if meatballs are frozen. Yield: 80 meatballs.

-Donna Weaver/Malinda Yoder/Naomi S. Gingerich

Escabeche (Belize)

3-4 c. chicken, boneless
8 c. chicken broth
1 Tbsp. oregano
2 bay leaves
2 whole cloves
2 Tbsp. recado (can
  substitute with paprika)

2 Tbsp. chicken soup
  base
Seasoning salt
2 hot peppers
3 large onions
1/2 c. vinegar
3 c. water, boiling

Place chicken and broth in a saucepan. Add oregano, bay leaves, cloves, recado, soup base and salt. Bring to a boil; then simmer gently. Meanwhile, slice onions and peppers, placing them in another pan. Pour vinegar and water over them. Let set for 5-10 minutes. Drain and add to boiling broth. Boil for 5-10 minutes. NOTE: Traditionally eaten by scooping the chicken and onion with fried tortillas and drinking the broth.

-Carol Miller

Best Meatloaf

1 1/2 lb. ground beef
  or deer meat
3/4 c. oatmeal
2 eggs, beaten
1/4 c. onion, chopped

2 tsp. salt
1/4 tsp. pepper
1 c. tomato juice
  or pizza sauce

SAUCE:
1/2 c. ketchup
1 Tbsp. mustard

2 Tbsp. brown sugar

Combine meat, oatmeal, eggs, onion, tomato juice, salt and pepper and mix thoroughly. Pack firmly into a 9"x9" loaf pan. Mix sauce ingredients together and pour sauce over loaf. Bake at 350° for 1 hour. Let stand 5 minutes before slicing. NOTE: To make hamburgers, omit eggs and reduce tomato juice to 1/2 c. or 3/4 c. depending on dryness of meat.

-Marilyn Hershberger

Meatloaf

2 1/4 lb. beef chuck
1/4 c. onions, chopped
1/2 c. oatmeal
1/3 c. milk
1 c. ketchup
3 eggs

1/2 c. bread crumbs
3/4 tsp. salt
1/4 tsp. pepper
2 Tbsp. parsley,
  chopped

SAUCE:
3/4 c. ketchup
8 tsp. prepared mustard

2 tsp. cider vinegar
8 tsp. brown sugar

Soak oatmeal in milk for 15 minutes. Add onions, 1 c. ketchup, eggs, bread crumbs, salt, pepper and parsley. Stir; add meat and mix thoroughly. Grease 2 mini or 1 large bread pan. Shape loaf (ves) in pan. Bake at 350° for 45 minutes. Mix sauce ingredients in a bowl. Brush sauce on top of meatloaf. Bake for an additional 5 minutes. Serves 8-10 people.

-Vicki Yoder

Potato Casserole

8 medium potatoes
2 lb. ground beef
Water

Flour
Salt (to taste)
Pepper (to taste)

Peel potatoes and put through salad cutter to slice. Cook meat in a skillet with plenty of water. Take cooked meat out of skillet and add to potatoes. Use the water in the skillet and add flour to make a thick gravy. Mix all together, adding salt and pepper. Pour into casserole dish and bake at 350° for 1 hour. Serves 8.

-Erma Hershberger

Meatloaf

2 1/4 lb. ground beef
2 eggs, beaten
3/4 c. cracker crumbs
Salt (to taste)
Pepper (to taste)
1 c. milk

2 bread slices, diced
1 Tbsp. minced onions
1/4 c. ketchup
2 Tbsp. butter
1/2 c. water

SAUCE:
1/2 c. ketchup
1 Tbsp. Worcestershire sauce
2 Tbsp. vinegar

4 Tbsp. brown sugar
1/4 tsp. Tabasco sauce
1 tsp. mustard

Combine cracker crumbs and eggs to soften. Place bread in milk. Combine meat, onions, 1/4 c. ketchup, salt and pepper. Mix well. Melt butter in bottom of a 9"x13" baking dish. Press meat mixture into 2 rolls. Pour water around meat. Bake at 350° for 1 hour. Cut meat into desired pieces. Mix sauce ingredients together and pour over meat. Return to oven for an additional 10 minutes.

-Elsie Schrock

Shepherd's Pie

1 lb. hamburger
1 small can mushroom soup
1/2-2 c. corn
6-8 cheese slices

4 or 5 medium potatoes, cooked and mashed

Brown meat and drain. Mix with mushroom soup; then place in bottom of a 2 qt. casserole dish. Spread corn on top of meat mixture. Place a layer of cheese over corn (save a few slices for on top). Make mashed potatoes and spread for next layer of casserole. Bake at 350° for 1/2 hour. Place last layer of cheese on top. Cover to let cheese melt, then serve. Serves 4 people.

-Beth Ernst

121

Herbed Meatloaf

MEAT MIXTURE:

1 lb. ground beef
1 lb. sausage or
  ground turkey
3/4 c. bread crumbs
1 c. milk
2 eggs, beaten
1/8 tsp. pepper
1 tsp. salt

1/2 tsp. sage
1/4 tsp. poultry
  seasoning
2 Tbsp. celery, chopped
1/4 c. ground onion
1/4 tsp. dry mustard
1 Tbsp. Worcestershire
  sauce

SAUCE:

3 Tbsp. brown sugar
1/4 c. ketchup

1 tsp. prepared
  mustard

Soak bread crumbs in milk. Add remaining meat mixture ingredients. Mix well and form into a loaf. Mix sauce ingredients together and spread over loaf. Bake at 350° for 1 hour. Serves 6 people.

-Lynette Miller

Company Stew

1 lb. stewing beef, cubed
4 large potatoes, cut into chunks
4 med. carrots, cut into chunks
1 c. celery, diced
1 small onion, chopped
1 tsp. salt

1/8 tsp. pepper
2 Tbsp. minute tapioca
10 oz. tomato
  soup (or juice)
10 oz. water

Place raw meat in bottom of casserole dish and top with raw vegetables. Sprinkle with salt, pepper and tapioca. Pour soup and water on top. [If using tomato juice, add 1 tsp. sugar.] Cover and bake at either 275° for 5 hours, or at 375° for 30 minutes plus 2 1/2 hours at 300°. NOTE: Vegetables, meat and gravy should all be a rich brown when done. If you trust your oven temperature, do not lift lid until done. Serves 6 to 8 people.

-Alma Spires

Beef Stew

14 1/2 oz. tomatoes, diced
1 c. water
3 Tbsp. quick-cooking tapioca
2 tsp. sugar
1 1/2 tsp. salt
1/2 tsp. pepper
2 lb. lean beef stew meat,
 cubed

4 medium carrots, cut
 into 1" chunks
3 medium potatoes,
 peeled and quartered
2 celery stalks,
 cut into 3/4" chunks
1 medium onion, diced
1 slice bread, cubed

In a large bowl, combine tomatoes, water, tapioca, sugar, salt and pepper. Add remaining ingredients; mix well. Pour into a greased 9"x13" baking dish. Cover and bake at 375° for 1 hour and 45 minutes - 2 hours, or until meat and vegetables are tender. NOTE: You can also put this into a crockpot on low for 6-8 hours. Serves 6-8 people.

-Becky Yerian

Cheeseburger Casserole

1 lb. ground beef
5 c. potatoes, peeled & sliced

Velveeta cheese, sliced

WHITE SAUCE:
1/2 stick butter
1/3 c. flour

2-3 c. milk
1 tsp. salt

Brown beef and drain off fat. Cook potatoes until tender. In greased 2 qt. casserole dish, layer beef, potatoes and cheese, repeating as necessary. Make white sauce as follows. Melt butter, add flour and stir. Add milk and salt then stir until medium consistency. [Works best if you microwave for 1 minute, stir, microwave for 1 minute, stir, and so on.] Pour white sauce over top of meat mixture. Bake at 325° until cheese is melted and bubbly.

-Kristi Gross

Igname Potato Casserole

An igname is a large tuber from West Africa

1 igname (or 6-7
  large potatoes)
1 onion-flavored bouillon
  cube, crumbled
3 c. vegetables, chopped
  (cabbage, carrots and zucchini)
Salt (to taste)
Pepper (to taste)

1 lb. ground beef
2 small onions,
  chopped
2 or 3 small cloves
  garlic, chopped
1 Tbsp. Worcestershire
  sauce

WHITE SAUCE:
3 Tbsp. margarine, melted
3 c. vegetable juice or water
1/4 c. flour
1/2 c. milk powder

1 tsp. celery salt
1/4 tsp. pepper
1/2 tsp. curry powder
1/2 tsp. paprika

CRUST:
3/4 c. milk
1/2 tsp. salt
1/2 tsp. baking powder

3/4 c. mayonnaise
3/4 c. flour

Boil igname (or potatoes). Grate. Add bouillon cube. Boil vegetables until tender. Saute meat with onions and garlic. Add Worcestershire sauce, salt and pepper. For white sauce, melt margarine in pan. Mix vegetable juice with flour and milk powder. Pour into margarine. Mix well. Add remaining white sauce ingredients. Bring to a boil, stirring constantly. To make crust, mix all ingredients together. Mixture will be runny. Layer the casserole in a greased 13" x 9" pan in the following order: vegetables, igname (or potatoes) and meat. Before pouring white sauce over this, punch some small holes through the meat and potatoes so white sauce gets down to the vegetables. Then pour white sauce over top. Spoon crust on top of white sauce. Bake at 350° for 1 hour. Serves 6-8 people.

-Sharon Gerber
(From friends in Burkina Faso, Africa, John & Carol Berthelette)

Plov (Kyrgyzstan)

1 medium onion
1 lb. beef, cut in small cubes
5 carrots, cut into julienne strips
1 lb. white rice
1/4 c. vegetable oil

Wash rice and leave it to soak in warm water. Cut onion into strips and saute in oil in a large, heavy pot over high heat, until golden in color. Combine beef with onions. Reduce heat and fry until well done, approximately 10 minutes. Add carrots and fry another 10 minutes, stirring constantly. Drain rice. Put rice into pot, on top of meat mixture. DO NOT STIR. Make rice level and add water to about 3 mm. above rice. Increase heat and leave pot uncovered. When water has dried up, put the lid on the pot and turn heat to low. Wait for about 40 minutes without opening lid. It's ready. You may eat. NOTE: Kyrgyz Rule of Plov: You must eat all that is prepared. It is not allowed, to leave a single grain of rice. Serves 6 people.

-Melissa Harrold

Taco Casserole

1 lb. ground beef
1 c. rice, uncooked
2 c. tomato juice
3/4 c. water
2 Tbsp. brown sugar
1 pkg. taco seasoning
2 c. cheddar
  cheese, shredded

Brown meat in a skillet. Add rice, tomato juice, water, brown sugar and taco seasoning. Simmer until rice is tender; add cheese. Serve with lettuce, tomatoes, sour cream and salsa.

-Carol Miller

Burger Bundles

1 c. Pepperidge Farm
  herb stuffing
1/3 c. water
3 Tbsp. butter, melted
1 lb. ground beef
1/3 c. evaporated milk

1 can cream of
  mushroom soup
2 tsp. Worcestershire
  sauce
1 Tbsp. ketchup
6 slices bacon
  (optional)

Combine stuffing, water and butter. Mix beef with evaporated milk and divide into 6 parts; flatten each into a 6" circle. Spoon "glob" of stuffing mixture on center of patty, draw edges over and bundle up. Wrap each bundle with a slice of bacon. Place bundles into baking dish. Combine mushroom soup, Worcestershire sauce and ketchup; pour over bundles. Bake at 350° for 45-50 minutes. Serves 4 people.

-Marjorie Weiss

Hamburger High-Hat

1/2 lb. bacon
1 lb. ground beef
1 large onion, chopped
1 can cream of chicken soup
1 tsp. salt
1/4 tsp. pepper
1/2 tsp. Accent flavoring

1/8 tsp. garlic salt
8 oz. Inn Maid
  Kluski Noodles
Poppy seeds, to taste
1 c. sour cream
2 Tbsp. butter

Cut bacon into small pieces; brown and drain. Brown ground beef and onion; drain. Add soup and seasonings to meat and heat until bubbling. Add sour cream and heat. Cook noodles according to package directions. Drain, then add butter and poppy seeds. Put noodles into greased 9"x13" greased pan; top with meat mixture. Sprinkle bacon on top. Bake at 350° for 15 minutes.

-Marjorie Weiss

Reuben

In the Round Crescents

16 oz. Pillsbury refrigerated
  crescent rolls
8 oz. pastrami, thinly-sliced
  or corned beef
6 oz. Swiss or mozzarella
  cheese, sliced

1 c. sauerkraut,
  drained
1/2 tsp. caraway seeds
1/2 tsp. sesame seeds

Separate 1 can of dough into 4 rectangles. Place into ungreased 12" pizza pan (or 9"x13" pan). Press dough over bottom and 1/2" up sides to form crust. Seal perforations. Arrange meat, cheese and sauerkraut in layers over dough. Sprinkle with caraway seeds. Separate second can of dough into 8 triangles and arrange spoke-fashion over filling, with points toward center. Do not seal outer edges of triangles to bottom crust. Sprinkle with sesame seeds. Bake at 400° for 15-25 minutes or until golden brown. Serve immediately. Serves 6-8 people.

-Ann Miller

Taco Tater Tot Casserole

1 lb. ground beef
1 medium green pepper,
  chopped
1 medium onion, chopped
Salt (to taste)
Pepper (to taste)

1 can tomato soup
7 oz. mushrooms
2 c. mozzarella
  cheese, shredded
1 pkg. Tater Tots

Brown ground beef, pepper, onion, salt and pepper together. Add tomato soup and mushrooms. Place in 9"x12" pan and add cheese. Top with a layer of Tater Tots. Bake at 400° for 30-35 minutes. Serves 6-8 people.

-Carol Miller

Mexican Casserole

6" flour tortillas
1 lb. ground beef
1/2 c. green pepper, chopped
1/2 c. onion, chopped
1 envelope taco seasoning mix
8 oz. tomato sauce
6 oz. tomato paste

1/4 c. water
1/2 tsp. chili powder
1 c. sour cream
2 eggs
1/4 tsp. pepper
2 c. corn chips, broken
4 slices Co-Jack cheese

Brown meat; saute vegetables until crisp-tender. Drain. Mix taco seasoning, tomato sauce, paste, water and chili powder. Bring to a boil and simmer for 20-25 minutes. Blend sour cream, eggs and pepper together in a small bowl. Place 2 tortillas on the bottom of a 9"x13" baking dish. Top with half of the meat mixture followed by half of the sour cream mixture. Place 2 slices cheese on top. Repeat layers with remaining meat, sour cream and cheese. Sprinkle corn chips on top. Bake at 350° for 25 minutes.

-Elsie Schrock

Simple Mexican Lasagna

1 pkg. flour tortillas
10 oz. refried beans
8 oz. sour cream

1 can enchilada sauce
2 c. cheddar cheese,
   shredded

In a deep dish pie pan, place 1 tortilla. Spread with refried beans, sour cream, approximately 1/4 c. sauce and a handful of cheese. Repeat this procedure several times until you have 3 or 4 layers. Bake at 350° for 30 minutes. When ready to eat, top each serving with sour cream. [You'll enjoy this so much you'll go out and buy more beans and enchilada sauce to make another one.] Serves 2 people. NOTE: Refried beans can be replaced with black beans. They are very tasty.

-Lynette Miller

Deep-Dish Taco Squares

1 lb. ground beef
1 medium onion, chopped
2 c. biscuit mix
1/2 c. water
1 1/4 c. pizza sauce

1 c. sour cream
2/3 c. mayonnaise
1 c. cheddar cheese
  shredded

Brown meat with onion; drain. Stir biscuit mix and water; line bottom of greased 9"x13" pan with the biscuit dough. Put a layer of meat mixture, then the pizza sauce. Mix sour cream and mayonnaise together and put on top of pizza sauce. Bake at 350° for 40 minutes. Put cheese on top. To serve, cut into squares. Serves 8 people.

-Carol S. Miller

Bubble Pizza

1 1/2 lb. ground beef
15 oz. pizza sauce
12 oz. refrigerated
  buttermilk biscuits

1 1/2 c. mozzarella
  cheese, shredded
1 c. cheddar cheese,
  shredded

In a skillet, brown the beef; drain. Stir in pizza sauce. Quarter the biscuits. Place in a greased 9" x13" dish. Top with the beef mixture. Bake uncovered at 400° for 20-25 minutes. Sprinkle with cheeses. Bake 5-10 minutes longer or until cheese is melted. Let stand for 5-10 minutes before serving. NOTE: Anything you like on pizza can be added to this. Part sausage and some pepperoni is a favorite. Serves 6-8 people.

-Gloria Gerber

Taco Pizza

1 1/4 c. cornmeal
1 1/4 c. all-purpose flour
2 tsp. baking powder
1 1/2 tsp. salt
2/3 c. milk
1/2 c. butter, melted
1/2 lb. ground beef
1/2 lb. bulk pork sausage
6 oz. tomato paste
14 oz. diced
  tomatoes, undrained
1/2 c. green onions, sliced

1 envelope taco
  seasoning mix
3/4 c. water
1 1/2 c. cheddar
  cheese, shredded
1 c. Monterey Jack
  cheese, shredded
2 c. lettuce, chopped
1 c. fresh tomatoes
  diced
1/2 c. olives, sliced

In a medium bowl, combine cornmeal, flour, baking powder and salt. Add milk and butter; mix well. Press into bottom and sides of a 12-14" pizza pan. Bake at 400° for 10 minutes or until edges are lightly browned. Cool. In a large skillet, brown beef and sausage; drain. Stir in tomato paste, canned tomatoes, taco seasoning and water; bring to a boil. Simmer uncovered for 5 minutes. Spread this mixture over crust. Combine cheeses and sprinkle 2 c. over meat layer. Bake at 400° for 15 minutes or until cheese melts. Top with lettuce, fresh tomatoes, olives, onions and remaining cheese. Serves 4-6 people.

-Christina Troyer

Pizza Pasta Casserole

1 lb. ground beef
1/2 large onion, chopped
28 oz. spaghetti sauce
8 oz. spiral pasta,
  cooked and drained

2 c. mozzarella
  cheese, shredded
4 oz. pepperoni, sliced

In a large skillet, cook beef and onion until meat is no longer pink; drain. Stir in spaghetti sauce and pasta. Transfer to a 13"x 9" baking dish. Sprinkle with cheese. Arrange pepperoni over the top. Bake uncovered at 350° for 35-30 minutes, or until heated through. Serves 8 people.

-Gloria Gerber

Pepperoni Pizza Casserole

4 oz. pepperoni, sliced
1 small onion, chopped
1/3 c. butter, melted
6 oz. spaghetti, cooked
1 c. Swiss cheese, grated
8 oz. mozzarella cheese,
  shredded

16 oz. tomato sauce
4 oz. mushrooms
1/2 tsp. oregano
1/2 tsp. basil

Boil pepperoni to remove excess fat; drain. Saute onions in 1/3 tsp. butter. Pour remaining butter into a baking dish. Add cooked spaghetti and 8 oz. tomato sauce. Add (in order) half of the Swiss cheese, half the pepperoni, half the mozzarella cheese, all the mushrooms and onions. Sprinkle with oregano and basil. Top with remaining tomato sauce, cheese and pepperoni. Bake at 350° for 20-25 minutes.

-Donnie Garner (First Baptist Church, Dover, OH)

Pizza with Hamburger Crust

1 lb. ground beef
1/2 c. dry bread crumbs
1 tsp. salt
1/2 tsp. oregano
8 oz. tomato sauce

8 oz. kidney beans,
    drained
3 slices cheddar or
    mozzarella cheese,
    cut into strips

In a large bowl, mix meat, bread crumbs, salt and oregano. Add 1/2 c. tomato sauce. Spread this mixture on ungreased 10" pizza pan (or on the bottom and side of a 10" pie pan). Add remaining tomato sauce and spread over meat mixture. Spread kidney beans over this. Arrange cheese strips in criss-cross design on top of beans. Bake uncovered at 425° for 20 minutes.

-Charlene Hunter (First Baptist Church, Dover, OH)

Ham Balls

1 lb. ground pork
1 lb. ground ham
2 eggs

3/4 c. milk
2/3 c. wheat,
    shredded, crushed

SAUCE:
1 1/2 c. brown sugar, packed
3/4 tsp. ground mustard

1/3 c. vinegar
2/3 c. water

In a bowl, combine pork, ham, eggs, milk and cereal; mix well. Shape into balls and place in greased 9"x13" pan. Combine sauce ingredients in a saucepan; bring to a boil over medium heat. Reduce heat and simmer uncovered for 4 minutes. Pour over ham balls. Bake uncovered at 350° for 60-70 minutes. Serves 8 people.

-Christina Troyer

Asian-Style Pork
An African Specialty

4 oz. spaghetti or rice
  noodles, cooked
2 c. pork, diced
2 onions, chopped
2-3 cloves garlic, chopped
3 c. vegetables (cabbage,
  carrots, peas, broccoli)

1/4 c. soy sauce
2 tsp. sugar
Salt
Pepper
Oil
Water

Fry diced pork in oil. Add some water and cook until done. Remove from pan. In the same pan fry onions and garlic. Add vegetables, salt and pepper. Saute until tender. Add meat, soy sauce and sugar. Mix and serve over noodles or spaghetti. Serves 4-6 people.

-Sharon Gerber
(John and Carol Berthelette, Burkina Faso, Africa)

Mountain Tribe Stir Fry
A Recipe from the Country of Laos

Oil
Pork (not lean)
Garlic
Ginger

Cabbage (cut in strips)
Rice
Salt (to taste)

In a cast-iron skillet, mince garlic and ginger and saute in oil. Cut pork into 1/2" cubes and cook in oil with garlic and ginger. Add salt. When pork is almost done cooking, add cabbage and stir until tender. Serve with rice. NOTE: This recipe underscores the simplicity of ingredients and the poverty of the mountain people in Laos.

-Noami Gingerich

Signature Dish (Laos)

2 lbs. ground pork or chicken
1 Tbsp. light soy sauce
1/3 c. cilantro, chopped
1/3 c. garden, chopped
  mint (not peppermint)
1/3 c. spring onions, chopped

1 c. glass noodles
Red peppers, fresh or
  dried and chopped,
  (optional)

Fry pork until cooked. Add remaining ingredients and simmer for a little while. Serve and enjoy! NOTE: Glass noodles are found in Asian grocery stores. To prepare them you need to soak them in hot water, then cut them into 1" pieces.

-Naomi Gingerich

Cabbage & Sausage

2 Tbsp. butter
1 c. onions
3/4 c. celery (optional)
3 Tbsp. flour
3 potatoes, dried
3/4 c. beef broth
1 tsp. thyme leaves, dried
1/2 tsp. Tabasco sauce

1 small head of
  cabbage, chopped
3 med. carrots,
  chucked
1 lb. kielbasa
  sausage, 1 in.
  pieces

Saute onions in butter; add celery. Stir in broth and flour. Cook 1 minute. Add thyme and Tabasco sauce. In a 3 qt. casserole dish, mix cabbage, carrots, potatoes and sausage. Pour broth mixture over cabbage mixture. Cover and bake for 1 hour and 15 minutes until vegetables are tender. Serves 6 people.

-Lori Day

Sausage Broccoli Manicotti

8 oz. manicotti shells
2 c. cottage cheese
10 oz. broccoli, frozen, thawed, chopped and well drained
8 oz. mozzarella cheese, shredded
3/4 c. Parmesan cheese

1 egg
2 tsp. parsley
1/2 tsp. onion powder
1 lb. bulk sausage
4 c. meatless spaghetti sauce
2 tsp. minced garlic
2 tsp. pepper
1/8 tsp. garlic powder

Cook manicotti shells; drain. In a large bowl combine cottage cheese, broccoli, mozzarella cheese, 1/4 cup Parmesan cheese, egg, parsley and other spices. Set aside. In a skillet cook the sausage until done; drain. Add sauce and garlic. Spread 1 c. meat mixture in a greased 9"x13" pan. Stuff shells with broccoli mixture. Arrange over sauce. Top with remaining sauce. Sprinkle with remaining cheeses. Bake uncovered at 350° for 40-50 minutes. Serves 6-8 people.

-Carol S. Miller

Grilled Swordfish

12-16 oz. fish
1 Tbsp. Worcestershire sauce
1 Tbsp. Dijon mustard
1 medium onion, chopped

1 clove garlic, minced
1/4 c. butter
Tabasco sauce (to taste)

Mix Worcestershire sauce, mustard, onion, garlic, butter and Tabasco sauce together. Cook fish in this sauce until tender. NOTE: This sauce is delicious and can be used with other white fish.

-Chris Bower

Miss Mandy's Stuffed Shells

1 lg. container cottage
  cheese or ricotta cheese
8 oz. cream cheese
2 c. mozzarella cheese
1 c. Parmesan cheese
2 eggs

1-3 cloves garlic
2-3 Tbsp. parsley
1 box large pasta
  shells, cooked
Spaghetti sauce
  or cheese sauce

Mix cottage cheese, cream cheese, mozzarella cheese, eggs, garlic and parsley in a blender or food processor until smooth. Using a Tbsp. stuff mixture into cooked shells. Place stuffed shells, stuffed side down into a 9"x13" pan. Cover with spaghetti sauce and serve with spaghetti sauce on the side. To make cheese sauce: Heat 1 pt. whipping cream or Half & Half in saucepan. Add 1/2-3/4 c. Parmesan cheese until thick. Pour over shells; bake 30 minutes at 350°.
Serves 12 people.

-Mandy Beachy

Deluxe Mac & Cheese

2 c. small curd cottage cheese
1 c. sour cream
1 egg, lightly beaten
3/4 tsp. salt
Garlic salt (to taste)
Pepper (to taste)

2 c. cheddar cheese
7 oz. elbow
  macaroni, cooked
  and drained
Paprika (if desired)

Combine cottage cheese, sour cream, egg, salt, garlic salt and pepper. Add cheddar cheese; mix well. Add macaroni and stir until coated. Transfer to a greased 2 1/2 qt. baking dish. Bake uncovered at 350° for 25-30 minutes. Sprinkle with paprika. Serves 8 people.

-Angie Peck

Italian Manicotti

4 c. ricotta cheese
2 c. mozzarella cheese, shredded
1/4 c. Parmesan cheese
3 Tbsp. fresh parsley, chopped
1 egg

1/2 Tbsp. salt
1/2 Tbsp. pepper
12-14 manicotti
  shells
3-4 c. spaghetti sauce

TOPPING:
1/2 c. mozzarella cheese, shredded

In a large bowl, mix cheeses, egg, parsley, salt and pepper together. Place in refrigerator for 15 minutes. Cook manicotti shells according to package directions. Rinse and drain pasta. Lay flat on a plate to cool. Spoon cheese mixture into cooled shells. Spread thin layer of sauce on bottom of 9"x13" glass baking pan. Arrange filled pasta in single layer over sauce. Pour remaining sauce over pasta. Sprinkle with Topping cheese and cover with foil. Bake at 350° for 40 minutes. Remove foil and bake 15 minutes longer or until bubbly. Serves 7-8 people.

-Tatiana Wilkins' grandma

Baked Spaghetti

16 oz. spaghetti
2 c. mozzarella
  cheese, shredded
3/4 c. Parmesan cheese
1/2 c. Romano cheese
1 tsp. garlic powder

3 eggs, beaten
1 Tbsp. olive oil
Salt (to taste)
Pepper (to taste)
28 oz. spaghetti
  sauce

Cook spaghetti; drain. Mix the cheeses together. Add 3 c. of cheese mixture to eggs, oil and spices. Press into a greased 9"x13" baking pan. Top with sauce. Cover and bake at 350° for 20 minutes. Uncover and sprinkle with remaining cheese. Bake 10 minutes longer until cheese is melted. Serves 8 people.

-Carol S. Miller

Baked Spaghetti

3/4 lb. spaghetti, cooked
2 eggs, beaten
1/2 c. butter, melted
1/2 c. fresh Parmesan
  cheese, shredded
1 container ricotta
  cheese
1 lb. and 10 oz.
  spaghetti sauce
2 c. mozzarella cheese

Rinse and cool spaghetti. Mix eggs, butter and Parmesan cheese together. Add to cooled spaghetti and stir thoroughly. Divide spaghetti into 2 greased pie pans. Cover each with ricotta cheese. Divide and spread spaghetti sauce evenly on top of ricotta cheese. Cover each with 1 c. mozzarella cheese. Cover with lid or foil and bake at 350° for 30 minutes.

-Louise Marner

Individual Ham Loaves

1 1/2 lb. ground fresh pork
1 lb. ground smoked ham
  or 2 1/2 lb. ham loaf mix
2 eggs, slightly beaten
2 c. Saltine cracker
  crumbs
1 c. milk

SAUCE:
2 tsp. dry mustard
3/4 c. brown sugar,
  firmly packed
1/2 c. vinegar
1/2 c. water

Combine pork, ham, cracker crumbs, milk and eggs. Shape into 10 loaves and place in a shallow pan. Blend sauce ingredients together and pour over ham loaves. Bake at 350° for 45-50 minutes. Baste loaves with sauce while baking. NOTE: To freeze cover baking pan with aluminum foil. Seal, label and freeze. To bake do not thaw. Bake uncovered at 375° for 1 hour-1 hour and 15 minutes.

-Dena Green

Baked Egg Casserole

4 eggs, deviled
1/4 c. butter
1/2 c. salt
1/4 c. flour
Salt water

2 c. milk, heated
1/2 lb. Velveeta
  cheese, diced
8 oz. medium
  noodles

Melt butter; combine with flour and salt. Add to milk and stir until sauce is smooth and thickened. Add cheese; stir over low heat until melted. (This can be done in a microwave.) Meanwhile, cook noodles in salt water until tender. Combine with half the cheese sauce and pour into a shallow, buttered 2 qt. baking dish. Nest egg halves in the noodles, cover with remaining cheese sauce. Bake at 350° for 20-30 minutes or until ingredients are thoroughly heated and top begins to brown. Serves 4-5 people.

-Gloria Gerber

Linguine & Clam Sauce

8 oz. linguine
4 Tbsp. butter
2 Tbsp. olive oil
4 cloves garlic
19 1/2 oz. clams,
  chopped & drained

1/2 c. Parmesan
  cheese, grated
1/4 c. parsley, finely
  chopped
1/2 c. Half & Half

Cook linguine according to package directions; drain. In a wide frying pan over medium heat melt butter in oil. Add garlic and cook, stirring, for 2 minutes. Add Half & Half and clams. Heat through but do not boil. Place hot linguine in a serving bowl. Pour clam mixture over top. Add parsley and cheese; toss until well combined. Serve immediately. NOTE: Our family likes to add mushrooms and green onions while frying the garlic - mmm good! Serves 4 people.

-Christina Troyer

Shrimp Jambalaya
Louisiana Cajun Style

2 tsp. butter
1 1/2 c. shrimp,
  cleaned & drained
1 onion, minced
1 green pepper
1 clove garlic, minced
1 c. white rice, uncooked
Tabasco (to taste)

1 tsp. salt
Black pepper (to
  taste)
Red pepper (to taste)
1 bay leaf
2 c. water
1/2 c. fresh mush-
  rooms, uncooked

In a skillet, melt butter. Saute shrimp; add remaining ingredients. Cover and cook until the mixture begins to steam. Turn heat down. Simmer and cook 30 minutes. Serve as a main dish with a large green salad and garlic rolls. NOTE: This was a favorite dish of ours until the kids came along. I occasionally make it as a special treat for my husband. Serves 2-3 people.

-Christina Troyer

Calico Beans

16-oz. pork and beans
16 oz. kidney beans
16 oz. butter beans
1/2 c. brown sugar
2 Tbsp. vinegar
1/2 c. ketchup

1/2 lb. bacon,
  cooked or
  bacon bits
1 small onion, chopped
1 lb. ground beef,
  browned

Drain beans. Combine all ingredients together and put into a casserole dish. Bake at 350° for 1 hour or place in a crockpot and cook for approximately 3 1/2 hours.

-Teresa Markley

Salmon & Rice

4 c. white or brown
  rice cooked
1 large can red or pink salmon

1 c. Velveeta, ched-
  dar or mozzarella
  cheese, shredded

SAUCE:
6 Tbsp. butter
4 Tbsp. flour

2 c. milk

Melt butter and stir in flour; mix well. Add milk and bring to a boil. Cook until it thickens. Place a layer of rice on bottom of a greased casserole dish; a layer of salmon, cheese and some sauce. Repeat layers. End with sauce. Cover with cracker crumbs and dot with butter then sprinkle with cheese. Bake uncovered at 350° for 25 minutes.

-Marilyn Hartman

Savory Lentils (Daal)
A Nepali Recipe

3 c. water
1 c. lentils, dried
1 tsp. salt
1 tsp. ground turmeric
1 medium onion,
  finely chopped

2 cloves garlic,
  finely chopped
1 tsp. ground cumin
1/4 tsp. ground
  cardamom
2 Tbsp. vegetable oil

Rinse lentils. Heat water and lentils to boiling. Stir in salt and turmeric. Cover and simmer until lentils are tender, approximately 45 minutes. Cook and stir onion, garlic, cumin and cardamom in oil until onion is tender. Stir into lentils. Cook uncovered over low heat, stirring frequently until consistency like refried beans, 20-30 minutes. Serve over rice. NOTE: Baby red lentils are very good to use!

-Tammy Koser

Grilled Salmon Sandwiches

8 oz. red or pink salmon,
  well drained
1/3 c. celery, finely chopped
2 Tbsp. sweet pickle
  relish, well drained
1/8 tsp. ground pepper

1/4 c. mayonnaise
8 slices white or
  Italian bread
1 egg, beaten
2/3 c. milk

Combine egg and milk. In a separate bowl, combine salmon, celery, pickle relish, pepper and mayonnaise. Divide and spread over 4 slices of bread. Top with remaining bread slices and dip each sandwich into egg mixture. Brown on both sides in a well-greased griddle or skillet. Serve immediately. Yields: 4 sandwiches

-Dean and Arvilla Kaufman

Orange Lentils

Musurko Daal from Nepal

1 c. orange lentils
1/2 tsp. salt
Water
2 Tbsp. butter

1/4 tsp. cumin
1/2 tsp. turmeric
  powder
1 onion, chopped

Wash lentils; cover with water and allow to soak for about 1 hour. Drain water. Boil lentils and salt in 1 1/2 c. water on medium heat for 45 minutes. Mix thoroughly with water. Heat butter in a skillet and fry cumin until black in color. Fry onion until it is golden. Add turmeric and stir. When lentils are tender add fried items and stir. Serve hot over rice. NOTE: Split peas may be substituted for orange lentils.

-Gopal and Sheila Sharma, Nepal

Indonesian Bamie

8 oz. vermicelli
5 Tbsp. vegetable oil
2 cloves garlic, minced
1/2 tsp. red pepper, crushed
1 lb. sirloin steak,
  thinly sliced
1/4 lb. shrimp

2 green onions
2 c. green cabbage,
  shredded
1/2 c. celery, sliced
  1/4" thick
1/4 c. soy sauce

Cook vermicelli according to package directions in boiling water. Drain; rinse with cold water and drain again. Set aside. Place a wok or frying pan over high heat and add 2 Tbsp. oil. When oil is hot add garlic and pepper then add steak. Stir fry 1 minute. Add shrimp and stir fry until meats are ready. Remove from pan. Pour 2 more Tbsp. oil in pan and add the vegetables. Stir fry until the vegetables are tender crisp. Add vermicelli, 1 Tbsp. oil and soy sauce. Stir fry 1 minute. Add meat and stir fry until most of the liquid has evaporated. Serves 4-6 people.

-Christina Troyer

Mexican Rice

2 c. rice
1 tsp. salt
1/4 c. onions, chopped
Vegetables of your
  choice (optional)

1 can corn
3 Tbsp. butter
3 Tbsp. vegetable oil
4 1/2 c. water

Put oil and salt into a frying pan. Add rice and onions. If desired, you can add other uncooked vegetables at this time. Fry for 8-10 minutes or until rice turns a light brownish color. Add 2 c. water and corn. Cover. Add more water, as needed, until the rice is cooked. Add butter and additional salt, to taste. Serves 6-8 people.

-Dayna Miller
(Linares N.L., Mexico)

Moroccan Tangine Stew

1 lb. lentils
2-3 lbs. beef, cubed
6 Tbsp. olive oil
2 onions, grated
2 garlic cloves, crushed
4 tomatoes, peeled,
  seeded and diced
Salt (to taste)
4 carrots, sliced

1/2 tsp. cumin
1/2 tsp. cinnamon
1/4 tsp. powdered
  ginger
1/4 tsp. sweet
  pepper
1/4 tsp. hot red pepper
Pepper (to taste)

Wash lentils and place in saucepan. Fill pan with water and bring to a boil. Remove from heat and soak lentils for 1 hour. Drain. Mix remaining ingredients and rub into meat. Put into a large saucepan and add water to cover. Bring to a boil. Skim, reduce heat to a simmer and cover saucepan. Cook until lentils are tender. NOTE: Delicious served piping hot on a cold winter day. To eat in Moroccan style, use bread to pick up the stew instead of using spoons. May be served individually but Moroccans like to eat it from a large shared platter.

-Phillip Martin
(Morocco)

Calico Baked Beans

1 can kidney beans
1 can butter beans,
  drained
2 cans pork and beans
1 c. brown sugar
1 c. ketchup

1 tsp. mustard
1 small onion,
  minced
1/2 lb. bacon, fried
  and crumbled
1 lb. ground beef

Brown ground beef and onion; drain fat. Mix all ingredients together and place in a casserole dish. Bake at 350° for 1 hour, or slow cook all day in a crockpot.

-Kathy Marner

Mexican Refried Beans

1 lb. pinto beans
1 garlic clove
2 tsp. salt
Water, boiling

3/4 c. vegetable oil
Cheese, shredded
  (optional)

*Place beans and garlic in water and boil for 2 1/2 - 3 1/2
hours. Add more water as needed. When beans are soft and
break open add salt; cook another 5 minutes. Remove beans
and put into a blender. Save water for adding as needed to
help blend beans. Heat oil in a frying pan. When hot, add
blended beans. Stir well until the oil is mixed into beans. Add
cheese on top. Serves 6-8 people.*

-Dayna Miller
(Linares N.L., Mexico)

Spinach & Rice

1 c. onion, chopped
1 c. milk
2 tsp. garlic, minced
2 Tbsp. canola oil
2 lb. fresh spinach or 10 oz.
  frozen and chopped
Dash of cayenne pepper
2 c. cheddar cheese, shredded

4 c. brown rice,
  cooked
2 Tbsp. parsley,
  chopped
4 Tbsp. soy sauce
4 eggs, beaten
1/2 tsp. salt

*Saute onion and garlic; add spinach and cook for 4 minutes.
Remove from heat and add remaining ingredients. Mix.
Spread into greased baking pan; sprinkle with paprika. Bake
at 350° for 35 minutes. NOTE: More soy sauce can be added if
desired. Serve with baked potatoes or fish. Serves 8 people.*
-Carol S. Miller

Indian Fried Rice

1 c. regular rice, uncooked
  (Basmati Rice is great!)
1 medium onion, chopped
1/2 c. margarine or butter
2 tsp. instant chicken
  bouillon

1 tsp. curry powder
1/2 c. raisins
1/2 tsp. salt
2 1/4 c. water, boiling
1/4 c. slivered
  almonds, toasted

Cook rice. In a skillet, stir rice and onion in butter until rice is yellow and onion is tender. Add raisins, bouillon, curry powder and salt. Pour into ungreased 1 1/2 qt. casserole dish. Stir in water; cover and bake at 350° until liquid is absorbed, approximately 25-30 minutes. Stir in almonds. Serve with chicken or lamb.

-Tammy Koser

Chinese-Style Fried Rice

2 c. water
2 c. minute rice
4 Tbsp. butter
3 Tbsp. soy sauce

2 eggs, beaten
1/2 c. onions,
  chopped

Bring water to a boil; stir in rice. Remove from heat. Cover and let stand for 5 minutes. Meanwhile, cook eggs in butter until set. Add onions and rice. Cook and stir over medium heat until rice and onion are lightly browned, approximately 5 minutes. Combine 1/3 c. water and soy sauce. Stir into rice and heat through. Serves 4 people.

-Lois Smith

Egg Rolls

1/2 head cabbage, shredded
1 small onion, shredded
2 carrots, shredded
1 pkg. egg roll wraps

1 lb. bulk sausage
1 c. cheddar cheese,
 shredded

Brown sausage. Mix sausage, carrots, cabbage, onions and cheese. Place 2 Tbsp. on egg roll wrap and fold corners diagonally, using flour/water glue, as directed on egg roll package. Fry egg rolls in cooking oil, turning once, until each side is lightly browned. Drain on paper towels. Makes 18-20 rolls.

-Lori Day

A bit of fragrance always clings
to the hand that gives you roses.
-Chinese Proverb-

Indian Mango Chutney

1 mango, coarsely chopped
1 c. raisins
1 c. brown sugar, packed
3/4 c. vinegar

1 jar crystallized ginger,
 finely chopped
1 clove garlic, chopped
1 tsp. salt

In a saucepan, mix all ingredients together. Heat to boiling; reduce heat and simmer uncovered until slightly thickened, approximately 45 minutes. NOTE: Great served with curry dishes.

-Tammy Koser

Paul's Barbeque Sauce

2 c. ketchup
1 c. white sugar
1 c. brown sugar
1 tsp. garlic salt
1 tsp. onion salt

1 Tbsp. Worcestershire
  sauce
1/2 tsp. pepper
2 Tbsp. vinegar

Mix all ingredients in a medium size saucepan. Boil until sugar dissolves.

-Andrea Hostetler

Grandma Grave's Barbeque Sauce

2 c. brown sugar
24 oz. ketchup
1/4 c. vinegar
1 Tbsp. A-1 sauce
1 Tbsp. Worcestershire
  sauce

1 Tbsp. yellow
  liquid mustard
1 tsp. lemon juice
1 tsp. garlic powder
1 1/2 tsp. onion juice
1/2 tsp. seasoned salt

Empty ketchup into 2 qt. saucepan. Rinse bottle with vinegar; add remaining ingredients. Bring to a boil; simmer uncovered for 5 minutes. NOTE: Keeps in refrigerator for several days in tightly closed container. May be used with pork, chicken or beef.

-Grandma Grave

Barbeque Sauce
For Barbequed Ham Sandwiches

4 c. ketchup
1/2 c. brown sugar
1/2 c. soy sauce
1/2 c. vinegar

2 tsp. dry mustard
2 tsp. onion powder
2 tsp. garlic powder
5 Tbsp. chili powder

Mix all ingredients in a saucepan; heat until sugar is dissolved. To serve with ham, pour over shaved ham and continue to heat until meat is hot throughout. Serve on buns or bread. NOTE: Other meats may also be used. Yield: 25 sandwiches.

-Lynette Miller

"Each day comes bearing its own gifts.
Untie the ribbons."
Ruth Ann Schabacker

Marinade For Chicken

2 c. vinegar
2 c. water
1/2 lb. butter
1/2 c. salt

5 Tbsp. Worcestershire
   sauce
1/2 tsp. garlic salt
1/2 tsp. pepper

In a saucepan combine all ingredients. Heat to boiling. Pour over chicken and marinate for 20-24 hours.

-Andrea Hostetler

Coney Sauce

2 Tbsp. butter or margarine
2 Tbsp. flour
1 lb. ground beef, browned
Brown sugar (to taste)

1/2 c. barbecue sauce
1 tsp. mustard
1 c. ketchup

Melt butter and add flour. Stir to make a paste. Add remaining ingredients and simmer. Serve over hot dogs. Serves 10 people. Yield: 10 qt.

-Naomi Gingerich

Alfredo Sauce

1 stick butter
3 Tbsp. flour
2 c. Half & Half
1 c. chicken broth
Salt (to taste)
Pepper (to taste)

1 tsp. garlic powder
2 Tbsp. cream cheese
2 Tbsp. Parmesan
  cheese
Meat of your choice

In a saucepan, melt butter and add flour. Stir; add Half & Half and chicken broth. Stir constantly with a whisk. Add cream cheese, garlic powder, salt and pepper. If sauce seems too thick, add more Half & Half. Cook pasta until done. Add meat and sauce. Serve with Parmesan cheese. NOTE: Heavy cream may be used instead of Half & Half but plain milk is not recommended. This sauce is also good for primavera dishes.

-Marilyn Hartman

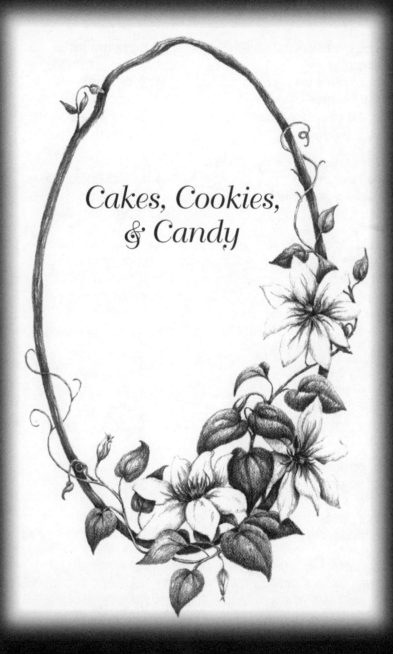

Cakes, Cookies, & Candy

Apple Pecan Cake

3 eggs, beaten
2 c. sugar
1/2 c. olive oil
2 tsp. vanilla
2 c. all-purpose flour
2 tsp. baking soda

2 tsp. cinnamon
1/2 tsp. nutmeg
1/4 tsp. salt
4 c. apples, diced
1 c. pecans, coarsely
  chopped

CREAM CHEESE FROSTING:
6 oz. cream
  cheese, softened
1/4 c. butter

1 1/2 c. confection-
  ers' sugar
1/2 tsp. vanilla

In a large bowl, beat eggs, sugar, oil and vanilla together. Combine flour, baking soda, cinnamon, nutmeg and salt. Mix into batter. Fold in apples and nuts. Spread into a 9"x13" baking pan. Bake at 325° for 50-60 minutes or until cake tests done. Cool. To make frosting combine all frosting ingredients in a small bowl. Whip until smooth and spread over cake. Serves 12-15 people.

-Dean and Arvilla Kaufman

Easy Apple Cake

2 c. apples, finely diced
1 c. sugar
1/4 c. vegetable oil
1 egg, beaten
1 c. flour

1 tsp. cinnamon
1 tsp. soda
1/4 tsp. salt
1 tsp. vanilla
1/2 c. nuts, chopped

Place apples in a mixing bowl. Add sugar and mix well. Let stand 1/2 hour. Add oil and egg. Blend. Add flour, cinnamon, soda and salt. Mix well. Add vanilla and nuts; stir. Bake at 350° for 45-50 minutes.

-Katie Miller

Dutch Apple Cake

2 c. sugar
1 c. vegetable oil
3 eggs
1 1/4 c. white flour
3/4 c. wheat flour

1 tsp. soda
1/2 tsp. cinnamon
4 apples, chopped
1 c. nuts

FROSTING:
6 oz. cream cheese,
  softened
1 tsp. vanilla

3 Tbsp. butter
Powdered sugar (as
  needed)

Mix sugar, oil and eggs together. Add dry ingredients, apples and nuts. Pour into a 9"x13" pan and bake at 350° for 45 minutes. To make frosting, mix cream cheese, vanilla and butter until smooth. Add powdered sugar until right thickness. Frost cake while still warm.

-Erma Yoder

Chocolate Cheese Cupcakes

1 box chocolate cake mix
8 oz. cream cheese
1 egg

1/3 c. sugar
1 c. chocolate chips

Make cake mix as directed on box. In a medium bowl, beat cream cheese, egg and sugar until smooth. Stir in chocolate chips. Place paper baking cups in cupcake pans and fill half full with batter. Spoon 1 tsp. of filling into each cup. Bake at 350° for 20-25 minutes. Yield: 36-40 cupcakes

-Joani Yoder

Apple Streusel Cake

STREUSEL:

1 c. light brown sugar
1 c. apples, chopped
1 c. almonds, pecans
  or walnuts, sliced

1/4 c. all-purpose flour
1 tsp. cinnamon
3 Tbsp. butter, melted

CAKE:

2 c. flour
1 tsp. baking powder
1 tsp. baking soda
1/2 c. butter, softened

1/2 c. white sugar
3 large eggs
1/2 tsp. vanilla
1/3 c. orange juice

GLAZE:

1/2 c. powdered sugar

2 1/2 tsp. orange juice

Preheat oven to 350°. Grease a 9" or 10" tube pan. To prepare streusel combine brown sugar, apples, nuts, flour and cinnamon in a medium bowl. Stir in butter. To make cake combine flour, baking powder and soda in a medium bowl. Mix well. With an electric mixer, using a large bowl, set on medium speed and beat butter and sugar until light and fluffy. Add eggs, 1 at a time. Beat well after each addition. Add vanilla. Set mixer to low; alternately, beat flour mixture and orange juice into the egg mixture. Spoon half of batter into tube pan. Sprinkle with half the streusel mixture. Spoon remaining batter over the streusel, spreading it to make an even layer. Swirl batter with knife to create a marble pattern. Bake for 15 minutes. Remove cake from oven. Sprinkle with remaining streusel mixture. Return cake to oven. Bake until a toothpick inserted in center comes out clean, approximately 30-35 minutes. Transfer to wire rack and cool completely. To make the glaze combine powdered sugar and orange juice. Mix well. Turn cake out onto serving plate; invert so streusel is on top. Drizzle glaze over cake and serve. Serves 12 people.

-Katie Barkman

154

Raspberry Crumble Coffee Cake

3 c. flour
1 Tbsp. baking powder
1 tsp. cinnamon
2 eggs, beaten
1 c. butter
1 tsp. vanilla

1 c. white sugar
1 tsp. salt
1 c. milk
1/2 tube of raspberry
  pie filling or 1 can
  raspberry pie filling

TOPPING:
1/4 c. butter
1/2 c. vanilla

1/2 c. white sugar
1/2 c. nuts

Combine dry ingredients together. Cut in 1 c. butter to form fine crumbs. Add eggs, milk and vanilla; mix. Spread half of the batter in a jelly roll pan. Put raspberry filling on top of batter. Drop remaining batter by small spoonfuls over filling and spread. Mix topping ingredients. Sprinkle on top and bake at 350° for 40-45 minutes. Optional: Make a glaze with powdered sugar and a little milk. Drizzle on top after it is baked.

-Erma Yoder

Lowfat Raspberry Cake

1 1/2 c. white sugar
2 eggs
1 1/2 tsp. soda
2 c. raspberries, fresh or frozen

2 c. flour
1 pinch salt, optional
1 c. milk, lowfat

Mix all ingredients together. Pour into a 9"x13" pan and bake at 350° until done.

-Carol Beachy

Best Ever Cake

2 c. flour
2 c. sugar
2 tsp. baking soda
1 c. walnuts, chopped

20 oz. crushed
  pineapple in juice
2 eggs
1 tsp. vanilla

FROSTING:
8 oz. cream cheese,
  softened
1/2 c. margarine, softened

1 1/3 c. powdered
  sugar
1 tsp. vanilla

Mix ingredients in order given using all of the pineapple juice. Use a wooden spoon for mixing. Bake in greased and floured 9"x13" pan at 350° for 45 minutes. While cake is baking, mix the frosting ingredients together. Beat until smooth. When cake is cooled spread frosting on top.

-Jacqueline L. Sherrell
(First Baptist Church, Dover, OH)

Peaches & Cream Cake

1 box yellow cake mix
30 oz. can peaches,
  drained
16 oz. cream cheese
1 c. sugar

2 or 3 Tbsp. peach
  juice
1 tsp. vanilla
Cinnamon
Sugar

Mix cake as directed on box. Place into a 9"x13" greased pan. Lay peaches on top of cake batter. Blend cream cheese, 1 c. sugar, peach juice and vanilla. Spread on top of peaches. Sprinkle cinnamon and sugar on top of cream cheese mixture. Bake at 350° for 1 hour. Serve with cool whip, ice cream or serve plain.

-Angie Gerber

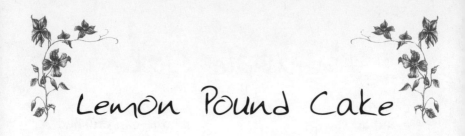

Lemon Pound Cake

2 c. sugar
1 c. butter or margarine
3 eggs
3 1/4 c. flour
1/2 tsp. baking soda
1 Tbsp. lemon juice, fresh

1/2 tsp. baking powder
1/2 tsp. salt
1 c. buttermilk
1 tsp. lemon rind, grated

LEMON GLAZE:
1/3 c. butter
1/2 tsp. lemon peel, grated

2 c. powered sugar
2-4 Tbsp. water, hot

Beat sugar and butter in a large bowl on medium speed until light and fluffy. Beat in eggs, 1 at a time. In another bowl combine flour, baking power, baking soda and salt. Stir well. Beat flour mixture into creamed mixture, adding alternately with buttermilk. Blend well. Stir in lemon peel and lemon juice. Spread batter in a greased and floured 10" tube pan. Bake at 325° for 1 hour or until wooden pick inserted halfway to center comes out clean. Invert on rack and remove from pan. Cool completely. Heat butter for glaze in a quart saucepan until melted. Remove from heat. Stir in lemon peel, powdered sugar and water until glaze can be dripped from spoon. Transfer cake to a serving plate, spread glaze over cake, allowing some to drizzle down sides.

-Evangeline Pryor
(First Baptist Church, Dover, OH)

Pineapple Cake

2 c. flour
1 c. sugar
2 eggs
1 tsp. baking soda

1 tsp. salt
1 large can crushed
   pineapple, including
   juice

1ST TOPPING:
1/2-1 c. brown sugar
1/2 c. walnuts

2ND TOPPING:
1 can sweetened
   condensed milk
1/2 stick butter
1 tsp. vanilla

Mix all ingredients together except the toppings. Pour into a 9"x13" pan. Sprinkle on 1st topping ingredients and bake at 350° for 30-40 minutes. While cake is baking, cook the 2nd topping ingredients together in a double boiler. Pour over cake as soon as it is removed from oven. Serves 10-15 people.

-Chris Bower

Moist Chocolate Cake

2 c. flour
2 c. sugar
3/4 c. cocoa
2 tsp. baking soda
1 tsp. baking powder

Pinch of salt
1/2 c. oil
1 c. hot coffee
1 c. milk
2 eggs

Mix eggs, oil, coffee and milk together thoroughly. Add remaining ingredients; mix well. Pour into greased 9"x13" pan. Bake at 350° for 35 minutes. Frost with your favorite icing.

-Geneva Schlabach

Chocolate Cake

4 c. flour
3 c. sugar
1/2 c. cocoa
1 Tbsp. soda

1 1/2 tsp. salt
1 c. cooking oil
3 Tbsp. vinegar
1 Tbsp. vanilla
3 c. water

In a large bowl, sift dry ingredients together. Stir in liquid ingredients. Pour batter in two 9"x13" greased baking pans. Bake at 350° for 30-40 minutes or until toothpick comes out clean.

-Loretta Hostetler

Pumpkin Cake

2 c. flour
2 tsp. baking powder
2 tsp. soda
1/2 tsp. salt
2 tsp. cinnamon

1 tsp. cloves, ground
2 c. sugar
2 c. pumpkin
4 eggs
1 c. vegetable oil

TOPPING:
1/2 c. butter or margarine,
   room temperature
4 oz. cream cheese,
   room temperature

2 1/2 c. powdered
   sugar
1/2 c. walnuts

Mix cake ingredients and pour into a bundt pan. Bake at 350° for 45-55 minutes. Cool. Remove from pan. Mix margarine, cream cheese and powdered sugar. Top cake with frosting. Sprinkle walnuts on top. Serves 10-12 people.

-Alma Spires

Heath Bar Cake

1 chocolate cake mix
1 jar butterscotch syrup
1 large container Cool Whip
1 can sweetened
condensed milk
1 pkg. Heath Bar Bits

Prepare and bake cake according to directions on box. While cake is still warm, punch holes with a wooden spoon. Pour syrup and milk over top, reserving 2 tsp. for garnish. Refrigerate until cold. Sprinkle with Heath Bar Bits, reserving some for garnish. Top with Cool Whip and garnish with syrup and Heath Bar Bits.

-Julie Hershberger

Ho-Ho Cake

1 chocolate cake mix

FILLING:
5 Tbsp. flour
1 c. sugar
1/2 c. shortening
1 1/4 c. milk
1/2 c. butter

TOPPING:
1 stick butter, melted
6 Tbsp. cocoa
2 Tbsp. water, hot
3 c. powdered sugar
1 tsp. vanilla
1 egg, beaten

Prepare cake as directed on box and bake in a 15"x10" pan for 15-20 minutes. To make filling cook flour and milk until thick. Allow to cool. Combine sugar, butter and shortening; beat until fluffy approximately 4 minutes. Add flour/milk mixture and beat another 4 minutes. Spread over cake. Mix topping ingredients together and beat until fluffy. Spread over second layer.

-Heidi Hershberger

Hot Fudge Pudding Cake

1 c. flour
3/4 c. white sugar
2 Tbsp. + 1/4 c. cocoa
2 tsp. baking powder
1/4 tsp. salt

2 Tbsp. oil
1 c. brown sugar,
  packed
1/2 c. milk
1 3/4 c. water, hot

Mix flour, white sugar, 2 Tbsp. cocoa, baking powder and salt. Blend in milk and oil. Pour into an ungreased 9"x9" pan. Stir brown sugar and 1/4 c. cocoa together. Sprinkle over batter. Pour water over batter. (NOTE: If you decide to use a smaller pan, cut back the amount of water.) Bake at 350° for approximately 45 minutes. The batter rises to the top and you have a really good fudge topping underneath. Serve warm with ice cream.

-Dena Green

Upside Down German Chocolate Cake

1 c. coconut
1 c. pecans, chopped
1 German chocolate
  cake mix

1 stick butter
1 pkg. cream cheese
1 box powdered
  sugar

Mix coconut and pecans together. Place in a greased 9"x13" cake pan. Prepare cake mix as directed on box. Pour over nuts and coconut. Melt butter and cream cheese together. Remove from heat. Add powdered sugar and beat until smooth. Pour over cake mixture. Bake at 350° for 35-45 minutes. Let cool completely. Easy and scrumptious.

-Marie Schrock

Chocolate Dream Cake

2 c. flour
2 c. sugar
1 stick margarine
1/2 c. Wesson oil
1 c. water
1/4 c. cocoa

2 eggs, slightly beaten
1/2 c. buttermilk
1 tsp. baking soda
1 tsp. vanilla
1 tsp. cinnamon

ICING:
1 stick margarine
3 1/2 Tbsp. cocoa
1 tsp. vanilla
1/3 c. milk

1 lb. powdered sugar
2/3 c. pecans
   (optional)

Sift flour and sugar in a large mixing bowl. Blend well. Add baking soda and cinnamon. In a saucepan bring margarine, oil, water, vanilla and cocoa to a rapid boil. Pour this mixture over flour and sugar mixture. Beat well. Combine eggs and buttermilk. Add all at once to batter, mixing well. Pour into a greased, lightly floured 9"x13" pan. Bake at 350° for 35-40 minutes. To make icing combine margarine, cocoa and milk in a saucepan. Heat slowly and bring to a boil. Add remaining ingredients. Beat well. Spread over cake.

-Marjorie Weiss

"Optimism is the faith that leads to achievement.
Nothing can be done without hope."
Helen Keller

Cinnamon Coffee Cake

1 1/2 c. flour
2 1/2 tsp. baking powder
1/2 tsp. salt
1/2 c. sugar

1/4 c. vegetable oil
1 egg
3/4 c. milk

TOPPING:
1/2 c. brown sugar
2 Tbsp. flour

2 Tbsp. vegetable oil
2 tsp. cinnamon

Mix flour, baking powder, salt and sugar; set aside. Mix oil, egg and milk. Add to dry ingredients. Mix topping ingredients. Pour half of batter in a 9" or 8" square pan. Put half of topping mixture on top. Add remaining batter, then top with remaining topping. Bake at 350° for 20-25 minutes. May drizzle with vanilla icing while still warm.

-Charlene Miller

Chocolate Bundt Cake

1 box yellow cake mix
1 small box instant
  chocolate or white
  chocolate pudding
1 c. almonds, slivered and
  crushed
12 oz. mini chocolate chips

8 oz. sour cream
4 eggs
1/2 c. oil
1 tsp. vanilla
1 tsp. rum flavoring

Mix all ingredients together and beat for 5 minutes. Pour into a greased bundt cake pan. Bake at 350° for 55-60 minutes. Let set 15 minutes. Turn onto cake plate. NOTE: If it sets more than 15 minutes it gets too difficult to remove! Sprinkle with powdered sugar or glaze when completely cooled.

-Marilyn Hartman

Delicious Dessert Cake

1 chocolate cake mix
14 oz. sweetened condensed milk
1 c. caramel sundae topping
2 c. Cool Whip
3 Tbsp. semi-sweet, sweet or milk chocolate, shaved

Prepare cake as directed on the package. Turn into a greased 9"x13" pan. Bake as directed. Cool. Punch shallow holes in the cake with the handle of a wooden spoon. Drizzle condensed milk over top. Spread with a rubber spatula to make sure it gets in the holes. Spread with caramel topping. Cover with Cool Whip. Sprinkle with chocolate shavings. Cut into 18 pieces.

-Becky Yerian

Honey Bun Cake

1 box yellow cake mix
4 eggs
4 tsp. cinnamon
3/4 c. oil

8 oz. sour cream
3/4 c. brown sugar
1 stick margarine,
   melted

GLAZE:
1 c. powdered sugar

4 Tbsp. milk

Combine cake mix, eggs, oil, sour cream and margarine. Pour half of batter into a greased 9"x13" pan. Mix cinnamon and brown sugar together. Sprinkle over batter. Pour remaining batter on top. Twirl with a knife. Bake at 275° for 50-60 minutes. Punch holes in cake while hot. Prepare glaze and pour over cake while hot.

-Larcie H. Vines
(Greenville, NC)

Florida Rum Cake

1 c. pecans, chopped
1 box yellow cake mix
1 box instant vanilla
  pudding mix

1/2 c. water, cold
1/2 c. dark rum

GLAZE:
1 stick butter
1/4 c. water

1 c. sugar

Place pecans in the bottom of a greased bundt pan. Stir cake mix, pudding mix, water and rum together. Mix well. Pour over pecans. Bake at 350° for 50-60 minutes. To make glaze boil butter, water and sugar together until sugar melts. Punch holes in cake while hot and pour glaze over top. Cool slightly then remove from pan.

-Marie Schrock

Rhubarb Coffee Cake

1/2 c. butter
1 c. brown sugar
1 egg
2 c. flour
1/2 tsp. baking soda

1 tsp. salt
1 c. buttermilk
1 1/2 c. rhubarb,
  finely diced
1 tsp. vanilla

TOPPING:
1/2 c. brown sugar
1 tsp. cinnamon

1/2 c. chopped
pecans

Cream butter, egg and brown sugar. Add remaining ingredients. Pour into a greased cake pan. Combine topping ingredients. Sprinkle on top of batter. Bake at 325° for 50 minutes. Serve warm with ice cream.

-Charlene Miller

Chess Cake

1 box butter flavored
  cake mix
8 oz. cream cheese
4 eggs

1 stick butter,
  softened
1 lb. powdered sugar

Combine cake mix, 1 beaten egg and butter together. Press into a 9"x13" cake pan. Beat 3 eggs and the cream cheese together. Mix in the powdered sugar. Pour over first mixture. Bake at 325° for 45 minutes.

-JoAnn Hershberger

Ivan's Carrot Cake

2 c. flour
2 c. sugar
1 tsp. baking powder
1 tsp. baking soda
1 tsp. salt
2 tsp. cinnamon

4 eggs
1 c. oil
4 c. carrots,
  shredded
1/2-1 c. nuts,
  chopped

FROSTING:
6 oz. cream cheese
4 Tbsp. butter
4 1/3 c. powdered sugar

1 tsp. vanilla or
  maple flavoring

Sift flour, sugar, baking powder, soda, salt and cinnamon together. In a separate bowl beat eggs until frothy; slowly beat in oil. Gradually add the flour mixture and beat until smooth. Mix in carrots and nuts. Pour into a greased and floured 9"x13" pan. Bake at 350° for 25-30 minutes. Blend cream cheese and butter and gradually add powdered sugar. Beat until thick and creamy. Stir in vanilla flavoring. Spread on cooled cake.

-Diana Henry

Buttermilk Sugar Cookies

2 c. white sugar
3 eggs
1 c. butter
4 1/2 c. flour

1 c. buttermilk
1 tsp. baking soda
1 tsp. baking powder
1 tsp. vanilla

ICING:
4 Tbsp. butter
1 lb. powdered sugar

Cream

Blend butter and sugar together. Add eggs, mix well. Add vanilla. Sift dry ingredients and add alternately with buttermilk. Bake 5-7 minutes in preheated 450° oven. (NOTE: It is important to use directed oven temperature, lower does not work.) To make icing mix butter and powdered sugar. Add cream as needed to get the moist consistency you want. Ice when cookies are cool.

-Marjorie Weiss

Sugar Cookies
(Quick & Easy)

4 c. flour
2 c. sugar
1 tsp. baking powder
1/2 tsp. salt
1 tsp. soda

1 c. vegetable oil
1 c. buttermilk
2 eggs
1 tsp. vanilla

Mix dry ingredients in a large bowl. Make a well in the middle of dry ingredients and pour liquids and eggs in the hole. Mix well and drop by tablespoons onto a cookie sheet. Sprinkle with sugar. Bake at 400° for 5 minutes.

-Malinda Yoder

Gingerbread

1/2 c. butter
1/2 c. white sugar
1 c. molasses
1 egg, beaten
1 1/2 tsp. soda
1 tsp. ginger

1 tsp. cinnamon
1/2 tsp. cloves, ground
1/2 tsp. salt
2 1/2 c. flour
1 c. hot coffee

Cream butter; add sugar and beat well. Add molasses and egg. Mix well. Sift together all dry ingredients. Add to creamed mixture. Mix well. Add hot coffee and mix. Pour into greased 9"x13" pan. Bake at 350° for 30-40 minutes. Serve warm with real whipped cream.

-Mary Ellen Troyer

Christmas Cookies
(Mrs. Mauk's Special Recipe)

1 1/2 c. sugar
1 c. butter, softened
1 c. sour cream
2 eggs

1 tsp. baking soda
1/2 tsp. baking powder
1 tsp. vanilla
4 c. flour

In a large mixing bowl, cream sugar and butter together. Add sour cream then eggs. Sift the dry ingredients together and add to creamed mixture. Add vanilla. Refrigerate overnight. Roll out on floured surface and cut with cookie cutters. Bake at 350° for 7-8 minutes. Yield: approximately 4 1/2 dozen cut-outs.

-Cheryl Miller

Christmas Cut-Outs

1 c. butter, softened
1 c. sugar
2 eggs
5 Tbsp. sour cream
1 tsp. vanilla

4 c. flour
2 tsp. baking powder
1 tsp. soda
1/4 tsp. salt

Mix butter and sugar. Add eggs, sour cream and vanilla. Add flour, baking powder, soda and salt. Roll out approximately 1/4" thick, cut with your favorite cookie cutter. Do not refrigerate. Dough should be room temperature. Bake at 350° for 6 minutes. Ice with your favorite icing. Yield: 4 dozen

-Mary Ellen Troyer

Soft Cut-Out Cookies

1 c. white sugar
1 c. brown sugar
1 c. margarine
3 eggs
1 c. heavy cream

1 tsp. salt
1 tsp. soda
5 tsp. baking powder
1 tsp. vanilla
5 c. flour

Combine sugars, margarine, eggs and cream; mix well. Add salt, soda, baking powder, vanilla and flour and mix well. Chill dough for a couple of hours. Roll out, using enough flour to make dough easy to handle. Roll 1/4"-1/2" thick and cut with a cookie cutter. Bake at 350° approximately 10-12 minutes or until lightly colored. Do not overbake!

-Alma Spires

Prizewinning Cookies

4 c. brown sugar
2 c. butter, softened
4 eggs
2 c. milk
1 tsp. salt
10 tsp. baking powder

4 tsp. soda
2 tsp. vanilla
1 tsp. nutmeg
9-10 c. flour
 (enough to make
 soft dough)

ICING:
9 Tbsp. sugar
6 Tbsp. milk
2 Tbsp. butter
1 tsp. vanilla
Pinch of salt

Pinch of cream of
 tartar
2 lb. powdered sugar
 (or enough to make
 right consistency)

Mix brown sugar and butter together. Add eggs, 1 at a time. Sift flour, salt, baking power, soda and nutmeg together. Add milk, vanilla and flour mixture to sugar mixture, slowly beating after each addition. Drop or roll out and cut. Bake at 350° for 7-8 minutes. To make icing combine sugar, milk, butter and salt in a pan and boil 2 minutes. Take off heat. Add cream of tartar. Stir really well. Let cool then add powdered sugar and vanilla until it is the right consistency to spread.

-Erma Hershberger

"Whatsoever thy hand findeth to do,
do it with all thy might."
Eccl. 9:10

Soft Sugar Cookies

2 tsp. baking soda
2 c. buttermilk
3 c. sugar
2 c. vegetable oil
2 Tbsp. baking powder

4 eggs
1 tsp. salt
3 tsp. vanilla
6 c. flour
Sugar

Dissolve baking soda in buttermilk. Set aside. Mix sugar, oil and eggs together. Beat well. Mix in baking powder, salt and vanilla. Alternate mixing buttermilk and flour into batter. Batter will not be real stiff. Drop by tablespoons onto greased cookie sheet. Place 6 Tbsp. separate on the cookie sheet. Cookies will spread out. Bake at 425° for 4-5 minutes or until golden brown. Take out of oven and sprinkle with sugar. NOTE: Colored sugar may be used for holiday cookies. Yield: approximately 40 cookies

-Sharon Gerber

Soft Sugar Cookies

1/2 c. butter or shortening
2 c. sugar
2 eggs
1 c. sour milk (see Note)
4 c. flour

1 tsp. baking soda
2 tsp. baking powder
1 tsp. vanilla
1/2 tsp. lemon extract
1 tsp. nutmeg

Cream the butter, sugar, eggs, vanilla, lemon and nutmeg together. Add the dry ingredients alternately with the sour milk. Chill dough overnight. Drop by teaspoons on greased cookie sheet. Flatten cookies with a juice glass dipped in granulated sugar. Bake at 350°-375° for 10-12 minutes, until edges start to brown. NOTE: You may add 1 Tbsp. lemon juice to sour the milk. Yield: 3-4 dozen

-Charlene Miller

Holiday Spice Cookies

1 c. unsalted butter,
  softened
1 c. brown sugar
1 c. white sugar
2 eggs
4 c. flour
2 tsp. baking powder

1 Tbsp. cinnamon
1 tsp. nutmeg,
  freshly grated
1/2 tsp. cloves, ground
1/2 tsp. salt
2-3 Tbsp. heavy
  cream, as needed

ICING:
1 lb. powdered sugar
2 egg whites

Food coloring
  (optional)

In a bowl with an electric mixer, cream the butter. Add the sugars, a little at a time, and beat the mixture until it is light and fluffy; do not overbeat. Add the eggs, 1 at a time, into a bowl. Sift flour, baking powder, cinnamon, nutmeg, cloves and salt. Add dry ingredients to the butter mixture and enough of the cream to form a dough. Divide dough in half. Form each half into a ball and transfer each ball to a sheet of waxed paper. Pat each ball into a 1/2" thick disc and wrap in waxed paper. Chill for 2 hours or overnight. Preheat oven to 350°. Line baking sheets with parchment paper. Let chilled dough soften to room temperature for 5-10 minutes or until it can be rolled. Roll out the dough between sheets of lightly floured waxed paper to a little more than 1/8". Dip desired cookie cutters in flour and cut out shapes. Arrange 1" apart on baking sheets. Bake for 7-8 minutes or until firm to the touch. Cool cookies on the sheets for 5 minutes and transfer to racks to cool completely. To make icing combine powdered sugar and egg whites in a bowl and beat with an electric mixer on low speed until sugar is completely moistened. Increase speed to high and beat 5 minutes or until icing forms stiff peaks. Color icing. Transfer to pastry bags fitted with small plain tips and decorate cookies. Cookies may be stored in airtight containers with layers of waxed paper in between for 2 weeks. Yield: approximately 3-4 dozen cookies (depending on size of cookie cutter).

-D Brown

The Best Chocolate Chip Cookies

2 c. sugar
2 c. Butter Crisco
4 eggs
2 tsp. vanilla
1 tsp. salt

2 small boxes instant
French vanilla pudding
2 tsp. soda
4-4 1/2 c. flour
2 c. chocolate chips

Beat sugar and Crisco until creamy. Add eggs and beat well. Add vanilla, salt, dry pudding mix and soda. Stir in flour, then chocolate chips. Drop by spoonfuls on lightly floured cookie sheet. Bake at 350° for 8-9 minutes. Do not overbake!

-Jayme Shaw

Chunky Mocha Cookies

1 c. shortening
3/4 c. white sugar
1/2 c. brown sugar, packed
2 eggs
2 Tbsp. milk
1 Tbsp. instant coffee granules
1 tsp. vanilla
2 1/3 c. flour
2 Tbsp. cocoa

1 tsp. soda
1/2 tsp. salt
1 c. pecans, chopped
1 c. semi-sweet
chocolate chips or
chunks
1 c. white chocolate
chunks

Combine shortening and sugars together. Add eggs, milk, coffee granules and vanilla. Beat well; combine flour, cocoa, soda and salt. Add to creamed mixture and stir well. Add pecans and chips. Drop by rounded teaspoonfuls on baking sheet. Bake at 375° for 10-12 minutes. Yield: 5 dozen

-Angie Peck

Chocolate Chip Cookies

3/4 c. Butter Crisco
1 1/4 c. brown sugar
2 Tbsp. milk
1 Tbsp. vanilla
1 c. Toll House semi-sweet
  chocolate chips
1 tsp. salt
3/4 tsp. baking soda
1 egg
1 3/4 c. flour
1 c. pecans, chopped

Combine brown sugar and Crisco in a large bowl. Beat until well blended. Add egg. Combine flour, salt and baking soda. Mix with creamed ingredients until blended. Stir in chips and pecans. Drop round teaspoonfuls onto ungreased cookie sheet. Bake 1 sheet at a time at 375° for 8-10 minutes. Cool before removing from cookie sheet. Yield: 3 dozen

-Kathy Torrence

Chocolate Chip Peanut Butter Cookies

1 c. butter, softened
1 c. creamy peanut butter
1 c. white sugar
1 c. brown sugar
2 eggs
2 1/2 c. flour
1 1/2 tsp. baking
  soda
1 tsp. baking powder
1/2 tsp. salt
2 c. chocolate chips

Cream butter, peanut butter, sugars and eggs together. Combine dry ingredients and add to creamed mixture. Stir in chocolate chips. Drop onto ungreased cookie sheet and bake at 375° for 9-10 minutes. Yield: 3-4 dozen

-Naomi Gingerich

Gingersnaps

3/4 c. butter or oleo
1 c. sugar
1/4 c. molasses
1 egg
2 c. flour

1 tsp. soda
1 tsp. baking powder
1/4 tsp. salt
1 tsp. cinnamon
1 tsp. ginger

Cream butter, sugar, molasses and egg together. Sift together flour, soda, baking powder, salt, cinnamon and ginger. Add to creamy mixture and mix well. Chill dough. Roll into walnut size balls, dust in white sugar. Bake on ungreased cookie sheet at 350° for 10 minutes. Yield: 5 dozen

-Jacqueline L. Sherrell
(First Baptist Church, Dover, OH)

Oatmeal Cookies

3 c. brown sugar
2 c. margarine
4 eggs
6 Tbsp. sour milk
6 Tbsp. molasses

2 tsp. soda
2 tsp. cinnamon
8 c. oatmeal
4 c. flour

Mix brown sugar and margarine until blended. Add eggs, sour milk, molasses, soda and cinnamon. Mix until blended. Slowly add flour and oatmeal. Drop onto ungreased baking sheet using a teaspoon. Bake at 400° for 12 minutes. NOTE: This is a double batch for large families, for small families cut the recipe in half.

-Andrew Brugger

Cake Mix Cookies

1 yellow pudding cake mix
1 egg
1/4 c. butter, melted

1/3 c. milk
1 c. chocolate chips
1 c. M&M's (optional)

Combine cake mix, egg, butter and milk. Mix until stiff. Stir in chips and M&M's. Bake on ungreased cookie sheet at 375° for 8-11 minutes. Let set a few minutes before removing from cookie sheet. To make bars press into a pan and bake for approximately 15-20 minutes and cut. Do not overbake. May substitute chocolate cake mix if desired. Yield: 3 dozen

-Carol Yoder

Ginger Cookies
(Aunt Mary's Special Recipe)

1 1/2 c. butter
2 c. white sugar
1/2 c. Brer Rabbit
  molasses (gold label)
2 eggs
3 Tbsp. applesauce

5 c. flour
4 tsp. soda
1/2 tsp. salt
2 tsp. cinnamon
1 tsp. cloves, ground
1 tsp. ginger

ICING:
6 Tbsp. butter
3 Tbsp. water, hot

1 tsp. vanilla
Powdered sugar

Cream butter, sugar, molasses, eggs and applesauce together. Mix well. Add dry ingredients and mix well. Chill dough for a couple of hours or overnight. Drop by teaspoonfuls on cookie sheet. Bake at 325° until done. Do not overbake. To make icing brown butter. Add water and vanilla. Thicken with powdered sugar until thick enough to spread.

-Christina Troyer

Peanut Butter Cookies

1 c. peanut butter
1 c. shortening or butter
1 c. white sugar
1 c. brown sugar, packed
2 eggs

2 1/2 c. flour
1/2 tsp. salt
1 1/2 tsp. soda
1 tsp. baking powder

Combine peanut butter, shortening and sugars. Beat until creamy; add eggs and beat. Add flour, salt, soda, and baking powder. Roll in balls. Press flat with a fork. Bake at 375° for 10 minutes. Do not overbake! Yield: 3-4 dozen

-Kathy Marner

Cornflake Cookies

1 c. white sugar
1 c. light Karo
1 c. peanut butter
1 c. pretzel sticks, broken

1 c. nuts
5 c. cornflakes

Mix sugar and Karo. Bring to a boil. Remove from heat. Add peanut butter and stir. Pour in pretzels, nuts, and cornflakes, mixing thoroughly. Drop by teaspoonfuls onto wax paper. Cool and eat.

-Kristi Gross

Monster Cookies

6 eggs
1 1/2 c. brown sugar
1 1/4 c. white sugar
1/2 tsp. vanilla
4 Tbsp. soda
1/2 lb. M&M's

1/2 lb. butter
1 1/2 lb. peanut butter
9 c. oatmeal
1/2 lb. chocolate chips

Cream eggs, sugars, vanilla, soda, butter and peanut butter together. Mix well. Add oatmeal and mix well. Add chocolate chips and M&M's. Scoop onto a cookie sheet with cream scooper. Bake at 350° for 12 minutes. Do not overbake.

-Summer Hershberger

Monster Cookies

6 eggs
2 c. brown sugar
2 c. white sugar
2 tsp. vanilla
1 Tbsp. Karo
4 tsp. soda

1/2 lb. butter or oleo
1 1/2 lb. peanut butter
9 c. quick oats
1/2 lb. chocolate chips
1/2 lb. M&M's

Beat eggs and sugars together. Add butter and peanut butter. Add vanilla, Karo, soda and oats. Mix well. Add chocolate chips and M&M's. Drop by teaspoonfuls on cookie sheet. Bake at 325° until lightly browned. NOTE: There is no flour in this recipe.

-Elsie Schrock

Snickerdoodles

1 c. shortening
1 1/2 c. sugar
2 eggs
2 2/3 c. flour

2 tsp. cream of tartar
1 tsp. soda
1/2 tsp. salt

Cream shortening, sugar and eggs together. Beat well. Add flour, cream of tartar, soda and salt together. Mix well then chill dough. Roll into balls and then into sugar/cinnamon mixture. Bake at 400° for 8-10 minutes on an ungreased cookie sheet.

-Andrew Brugger

Rhubarb Squares

2 c. + 4 Tbsp. flour
8 Tbsp. + 1 1/2 c. sugar
1 c. butter or margarine
1 c. milk
4 1/2 c. rhubarb, diced

4 egg yolks, beaten
4 egg whites, beaten
1/4 tsp. cream of
 tartar

Mix 2 c. flour, 4 Tbsp. sugar and butter. Press into a 9"x13" pan and bake at 350° for approximately 30 minutes or until light brown. Mix 4 Tbsp. flour, 1 1/2 c. sugar, milk and rhubarb in a saucepan and cook on medium heat. Stir constantly until the rhubarb is soft. Add egg yolks to rhubarb mixture. Cook until thick. Cool a little and pour on baked crust. Combine egg whites with cream of tartar and 4 Tbsp. sugar. Place on top of the rhubarb and bake until egg white mixture is golden brown on top. Serves 10-12 people.

-Alma Spires

179

Cashew Cookies

1 c. butter
3/4 c. brown sugar
1/2 c. white sugar
1 egg
1/2 tsp. cream of tartar

1/2 tsp. baking soda
2 1/4 c. flour
1 1/2 c. cashews,
   broken
1 tsp. vanilla

Cream butter and sugars together. Add egg and vanilla. In a separate bowl mix cream of tartar and baking soda together. Add to the first mixture. Add flour. Mix thoroughly. Stir in cashews. Bake at 350° for 10-12 minutes. Yield: 2 dozen

-Gloria Gerber

Refrigerator Cookies

1 1/2 c. sugar
1 c. margarine
1/2 tsp. salt
1 tsp. baking powder

2 eggs
1 1/2 tsp. vanilla
3 1/4 c. flour
Food colors

Beat margarine and sugar together. Add eggs and vanilla. Sift flour, salt and baking powder together. Add to first mixture. Once mixed, break into smaller portions and color with different food colors. Make into rolls 1" in diameter. Place rolls onto wax paper and refrigerate at least 1 hour. Place on greased cookie sheets and bake at 400° for 7-10 minutes or until they start to brown. NOTE: Works best if you double the recipe so more colors can be used.

-Andrew Brugger

Chocolate Walnut Sensations

1 c. + 2 Tbsp. flour
1/2 tsp. baking soda
1/2 tsp. salt
3/4 c. brown sugar,
  packed
1/2 c. butter, softened

1 tsp. vanilla
1 egg
12 oz. chocolate
  chips
1 c. nuts, chopped
  (optional)

In a small bowl, combine flour, soda and salt. Set aside. Beat brown sugar, butter and vanilla until creamy. Beat in egg. Gradually add flour mixture. Stir in 1 1/2 c. chocolate chips and nuts. Spread into a greased 9"x13" pan and bake at 375° for 23-25 minutes. Immediately sprinkle remaining 2/3 c. of chocolate chips on top. When soft spread smoothly over bars. Garnish with nuts. Yield: 24 pieces

-Chris Bower

Chocolate Caramel Bars

1 bag caramels
1 c. chocolate chips
1 German chocolate cake mix

1 small can
  evaporated milk
2/3 c. margarine

Combine cake mix, margarine and 1/3 c. of evaporated milk. Put half the mixture into a greased 9"x13" cake pan. Bake at 350° for 6 minutes. Let cool for a few minutes. Sprinkle chocolate chips over top. Combine 1/3 c. evaporated milk and caramels in a bowl. Microwave until melted. Spread over the top. Cover caramel mixture with remaining cake mixture. Bake at 350° for 18 minutes.

-Heidi Smith

Cherry Nut Cookies

1 c. butter
2 c. brown sugar
2 eggs
2 tsp. vanilla
4 c. flour
1 tsp. soda
1/2 tsp. salt
1 pkg. walnuts, chopped
1/2 c. maraschino cherries, chopped

Cream butter and brown sugar together. Add eggs and vanilla; beat until smooth. Blend in flour, soda and salt. Stir in walnuts and cherries. Form into 2" long rolls; wrap in wax paper and chill. Cut into 1/4" slices when ready to bake. Place on an ungreased baking sheet. Bake at 375° for 8-10 minutes or until brown.

-Teresa Markley

Chocolate Chip Cheesecake Bars

2 pkg. ready-made Pillsbury chocolate chip cookie dough
16 oz. cream cheese
2 tsp. vanilla
2 eggs
1 1/2 c. sugar

Press 1 pkg. cookie dough into an ungreased 9"x13" pan. Mix cream cheese, vanilla, eggs and sugar together. Pour on top of cookie dough in pan and crumble remaining cookie dough on top of mixture. Bake at 350° for 45 minutes. Cut in small pieces. NOTE: It is very rich.

-Lynette Miller

Granola Bars

1/2 c. butter
15 c. marshmallows
1/4 c. oil
1/2 c. honey
1 c. graham crackers,
 crushed

1/2 c. wheat germ
1 c. coconut
6 c. quick oatmeal
9 c. Rice Chex cereal
 (measure cereal
 first, then crush)

*Melt butter and marshmallows together. Add oil and honey.
Set aside. In a large bowl mix the remaining ingredients
together and pour the marshmallow mixture over it. Stir well
and press into a buttered cake pan. NOTE: No need to
bake this.*

-Carol Miller

Cheesecake Squares

32 oz. cream cheese,
 softened
2 c. sugar
4 eggs
1 c. plain yogurt

4 tsp. vanilla
2 tsp. lemon juice
1 c. buttermilk
 Bisquick mix

TOPPING:
2 c. sour cream
4 Tbsp. sugar

4 tsp. vanilla

*In a mixing bowl, beat cream cheese and sugar. Add eggs,
yogurt, vanilla, lemon juice and Bisquick mix. Stir just until
smooth. Pour into a 9"x13" baking pan. Bake at 350° for 45
minutes or until center is nearly set. Place on wire rack while
preparing topping. Combine sour cream, sugar and vanilla
until smooth. Spread on cheesecake. Bake for 8 minutes
longer. Cool, refrigerate and garnish with fruit. Serves
9 people.*

-Carol S. Miller

Pecan Fingers

3/4 c. butter, softened
3/4 c. powdered sugar
1 1/2 c. flour
2 eggs
1 c. brown sugar

2 Tbsp. flour
1/2 tsp. baking powder
1/2 tsp. salt
1/2 tsp. vanilla
1 c. pecans, chopped

Cream butter and powdered sugar. Add flour. Press evenly in the bottom of an ungreased 9"x13" baking pan. Bake at 350° for 12-15 minutes. Mix remaining ingredients. Spread over hot baked layer and bake 20 minutes longer. Cool. Cut into bars, approximately 3"x1". Yield: 32 bars

-Gloria Gerber

Peanut Butter Fingers

1/2 c. butter
1/2 c. white sugar
1/2 c. brown sugar
1 egg
1/3 c. peanut butter
1/2 tsp. soda

1/4 tsp. salt
1/2 tsp. vanilla
1 c. flour
1 c. oats
1 c. chocolate chips

GLAZE:
1/2 c. powdered sugar
1/4 c. peanut butter

2-4 Tbsp. milk

Combine butter and sugars together. Add egg, peanut butter, soda, salt and vanilla. Mix well. Add flour and oats. Spread in a 9"x13" pan. Bake at 350° for 20-25 minutes. Sprinkle chocolate chips on top while hot and let set 5 minutes. To make glaze combine powdered sugar, peanut butter and milk. Mix well and drizzle on top of bars. Cool and cut into bars. NOTE: This is a Dart Ball team favorite.

-Donna Weaver

184

Pumpkin Pie Squares

CRUST:

1 1/2 c. flour
3/4 c. quick oatmeal

3/4 c. butter
3/4 c. brown sugar

Mix ingredients together and press into an ungreased 9"x13" pan. Bake at 350° for 10-15 minutes.

FILLING:

2 c. pumpkin
1 c. Carnation milk
1 c. milk
3 eggs, beaten
3/4 c. brown sugar

1 tsp. cinnamon
3/4 tsp. salt
3/4 tsp. nutmeg
3/4 tsp. allspice

Mix ingredients well and pour on crust. Bake for 30 minutes longer.

TOPPING:

3 Tbsp. butter, melted
3/4 c. brown sugar

1/2 c. pecans,
   chopped

Mix together and sprinkle on top of filling. Put under broiler until slightly brown.

-Elsie Schrock

Buckeyes

1 c. butter or margarine
1 1/2 c. peanut butter

Chocolate
4 c. powdered sugar

Combine butter, powdered sugar and peanut butter together and mix well. Form into balls and refrigerate overnight. Melt chocolate and dip peanut butter balls into the hot chocolate, using toothpicks. Place balls on waxed paper until chocolate hardens. Enjoy!

-Alma Spires

Lemon Cheese Bars

1 box yellow cake mix
1/3 c. oil
1/3 c. sugar
2 eggs

8 oz. cream
  cheese, softened
2 Tbsp. lemon juice

In a large bowl, combine dry cake mix, 1 beaten egg and oil. Mix until crumbly. Reserve 1 c. crumbs. Press the remaining crumbs into an ungreased pan. Bake at 350° for 15 minutes. In a separate bowl, beat cream cheese, lemon juice and 1 beaten egg until smooth. Spread this mixture over crumb layer. Sprinkle reserved crumbs on top. Bake at 350° for 20 more minutes.

-Carol S. Miller

Frosted Pumpkin Bars

4 eggs, beaten
1 c. salad oil
1 c. pumpkin
2 c. sugar
1/2 tsp. salt

2 tsp. cinnamon
1 tsp soda
1 tsp. baking powder
2 c. flour
1 c. nuts, chopped

FROSTING:
6 Tbsp. butter or margarine,
  melted
3 oz. cream cheese, softened
3 3/4 c. powdered sugar

2 Tbsp. milk or
  orange juice
1 tsp. vanilla

Mix eggs, oil, pumpkin, sugar, salt, cinnamon, soda, baking powder and flour together. Mix well and add nuts. Pour into cookie sheet with sides and bake at 350° for 20-25 minutes. To make frosting mix butter, cream cheese, powdered sugar, milk and vanilla together until smooth. Frost bars while warm and cut into squares when cooled. Serves 10-12 people.

-Alma Spires

Nutmeg Butter Fingers

1 c. butter
3/4 c. sugar
1 egg

2 tsp. vanilla
3 c. flour
3/4 tsp. nutmeg

ICING:
2 Tbsp. light cream
1/3 c. butter
1 tsp. vanilla

1 tsp. rum flavoring
2 c. powdered sugar
Nutmeg

Cream butter and sugar until light and fluffy. Add egg, vanilla, flour and nutmeg. Mix well and shape into fingers on slightly buttered cookie sheet. Bake at 350° for 13-15 minutes. NOTE: They all fit on one cookie sheet. To make icing mix icing ingredients together and beat until smooth. Ice cookies when cooled. NOTE: It is important only to use butter. Makes a nice "short" cookie.

-Marilyn Hartman

Mocha Truffles

24 oz. chocolate chips
8 oz. cream cheese
3 Tbsp. instant coffee granules
1 lb. dark chocolate coating

2 tsp. water
1/4 lb. white
chocolate coating

Melt chocolate chips in a double boiler over low heat. When soft add cream cheese, coffee granules and water. Mix well. Chill until firm enough to shape. Roll into 3/4" balls and place on a cookie sheet lined with wax paper. Chill 2 hours. Melt dark chocolate coating and mix. Dip balls and place on wax paper until firm. Melt white coating, mix and drizzle on with cake decorater bag.

-Charlene Miller

187

Caramalitas

1 c. + 1 Tbsp. flour
1 c. quick-cooking oats
3/4 c. brown sugar, packed
1/2 tsp. soda
1/4 tsp. salt
3/4 c. butter or
  margarine, melted

1 c. semisweet
  chocolate chips
12 oz. caramel
  ice cream topping
1/2 c. walnuts,
  chopped

In a bowl, combine 1 c. flour, oats, brown sugar, soda and salt. Stir in butter; mix well. Press into a 9"x13" greased baking pan. Bake at 350° for 10 minutes. Sprinkle with chocolate chips. Combine caramel topping and remaining flour. Drizzle over chips. Sprinkle walnuts on top. Bake at 350° for 22 minutes.

-Carol S. Miller

Chocolate Yummies No-Bake

1 c. chocolate chips,
  semisweet
1/3 c. butter
16 large marshmallows

2 c. quick oats
1 c. coconut, flaked
1/2 tsp. vanilla

In a saucepan, melt chocolate chips, butter and marshmallows over low heat until smooth. Stir in oats, coconut and vanilla; mix well. Drop by rounded teaspoons on wax paper-lined cookie sheets. Chill until set, 30 minutes. Yield: 4 dozen

-Carol S. Miller

Sugar-Coated Pecans

1 Tbsp. egg white
2 c. pecans, halved

1/4 c. white sugar
2 tsp. cinnamon

In a bowl, beat egg white until foamy; add pecans and toss until well coated. In a separate bowl, combine sugar and cinnamon. Sprinkle over pecans and toss to coat. Spread in a single layer on an ungreased baking sheet. Bake at 300° for 30 minutes. Take spoon and mix pecans about every 10 minutes so they do not stick together. Cool on wax paper. Yield: 3 c.

-Katie Barkman

Uzbekistan Sweet Walnut Brittle

8 oz. light brown sugar
1/2 tsp cinnamon, ground
1/4 tsp. allspice, ground
1/4 tsp ginger, ground

3 oz. evaporated milk
12 oz. walnuts
1/2 tsp. vanilla
  essence

Place brown sugar, cinnamon, allspice, ginger and evaporated milk in a heavy saucepan and stir over high heat for approximately 5 minutes, or until sugar dissolves and the mixture reaches soft ball stage (115°c /238°f on sugar thermometer). Remove the pan from the heat and stir in the nuts and vanilla essence. Make sure all the nuts are coated. Pour out into a sheet of grease proof paper. Allow to cool then break into chunks. Store in an airtight container.

-Lewis Kaufman

"By watering others,
you water yourself."

-Proverbs-

Pies and
Pastries

Lemon Supreme Pie

9" graham cracker crust
1 can Thank You lemon
  pie filling
8 oz. cream cheese, softened

3/4 c. powdered
  sugar
Cool Whip or
  whipped cream

Beat cream cheese and powdered sugar together until smooth. Spread evenly on the bottom of pie crust. Spread pie filling over cream cheese layer. Top with Cool Whip.

Mrs. Evelyn Mills
(First Baptist Church, Dover, OH)

"What do we live for if not to make life
less difficult for each other?"

-George Eliot

Pineapple Fluff Pie

20 oz. crushed, unsweetened
  pineapple, drained
3.4 oz. instant lemon
  pudding

8 oz. Cool Whip
9" graham cracker
  crust

Mix pineapple and pudding until thickened. Fold in Cool Whip. Spoon into crust. Refrigerate. Serves 8 people.

-Carol S. Miller

Peaches & Cream Pie

CRUST:

3/4 c. flour
1 tsp. baking powder
1/2 tsp. salt
3 oz. vanilla pudding,
   not instant

3 Tbsp. margarine,
   softened
1 egg
1/2 c. milk

FILLING:

29 oz. peaches,
   sliced and drained
3 Tbsp. peach juice

8 oz. cream cheese,
   softened
1/2 c. sugar

TOPPING:

1 Tbsp. sugar

1/2 tsp. cinnamon

*To make crust, combine crust ingredients together and beat
with a mixer for 2 minutes. Pour into a greased 9" pie pan.
Set aside. To make filling place peaches in crust. In a separate
bowl combine cream cheese, sugar and peach juice. Spoon
over top of peaches to within 1" of edge of the dish. To make
topping, mix cinnamon and sugar together. Sprinkle over pie.
Bake at 350° for 35-40 minutes. Refrigerate and serve cold.
Must be prepared several hours ahead. Serves 8 people.*

-Marea Andreas

Lime Yogurt Pie

3 oz. lime gelatin
9" graham cracker crust

12 oz. key lime yogurt
8 oz. Cool Whip

*Combine gelatin and yogurt. Fold in Cool Whip. Spread into
crust. Refrigerate 20 minutes. Serves 6 people.*

-Carol S. Miller

Crusty Peach "Crustard" Pie

1 pie crust, unbaked
3-4 large peaches, fresh
1/2 c. flour
1 1/2 c. sugar

1/3 c. margarine
1 egg
1/2 tsp. vanilla

Peel and cut peaches in thick slices. Place pie crust in pan and lay peach slices in a single layer in pie crust. Crumb flour, sugar and margarine together. Add egg and vanilla. Spoon on top of peaches. Bake at 425° for 15 minutes; reduce temperature to 375° and bake for 40-45 more minutes. Serves 8 people.

-Vicki Yoder

Fresh Blackberry Pie

2-9" pie crusts, unbaked
1 1/4 c. sugar

1/2 c. all-purpose flour
4 c. blackberries
2 Tbsp. butter

Line pie pan with a pie shell. In a bowl, stir sugar and flour together. Carefully add blackberries and mix. Pour into pie crust. Dot with butter. Cut slits in 2nd pie crust. Cover pie with this crust and seal. Cover edge with 2-3" strips of aluminum foil to prevent excessive browning. Bake at 425° for 35-40 minutes or until juice begins to bubble through slits in crust. Remove foil for the last 15 minutes of baking. Cool. Serves 6-8 people.

-Tatiana Wilkins

Raspberry Cream Pie

1 can Eagle Brand milk
1/3 c. lemon juice
1/2 box black raspberry jello

1 1/2 c. raspberries
8 oz. Cool Whip
2 pie crusts, baked

Mix milk, lemon juice and jello together. Add raspberries and Cool Whip. Pour into pie crusts and top with Cool Whip. Yield: 2 pies

-Malinda Yoder

Blueberry Sour Cream Pie

1 c. sugar
1/2 tsp. salt
1/4 c. flour
2 eggs
2 c. sour cream
3/4 tsp. vanilla

1 can blueberry pie
  filling
1 c. whipped cream
9" graham cracker
  crust, unbaked

In a mixing bowl, combine sugar, salt, flour, eggs, sour cream and vanilla; mix well. Pour into a pie crust and bake at 350° for 30 minutes or until center is set. Pour filling on top of hot pie. Chill for several hours. Top with whipped cream.

-Carol S. Miller

Fresh Peach Pie

3/4 c. sugar
2 Tbsp. cornstarch
1 c. water

1/2 box peach jello
3 c. peaches, sliced
Pie crust

Combine sugar, cornstarch and water in a saucepan. Cook until clear. Add peach jello and cool. Add peaches to jello mixture. Pour into pie crust and chill.

-Katheryn Miller

Caramel Pear Pie

6 c. ripe pears, sliced
  and peeled
1 Tbsp. lemon juice
1/2 c. + 3 Tbsp. sugar
2 Tbsp. quick-cooking
  tapioca
3/4 tsp. cinnamon
1/4 tsp. salt
1/4 tsp. nutmeg

9" pie crust, unbaked
3/4 c. old-fashioned
  oats
1 Tbsp. flour
1/4 c. butter, cold
18 caramels
5 Tbsp. milk
1/4 c. pecans,
  chopped

In a large bowl, combine pears and lemon juice. In a separate bowl, combine 1/2 c. sugar, tapioca, cinnamon, salt and nutmeg. Add pears and stir gently. Let stand for 15 minutes. Pour into pie crust. In another bowl, combine oats, flour and 3 Tbsp. sugar. Cut in butter until crumbly. Sprinkle over pears. Bake at 400° for 45 minutes. Meanwhile, in a saucepan over low heat, melt caramels with milk. Stir until smooth; add pecans. Drizzle over pie. Bake 8-10 minutes longer or until crust is golden brown and filling is bubbly. Cool on a wire rack. Serves 6-8 people.

NOTE: This pie won 4th place out of 22 pies at the annual Charm Days Pie Baking Contest. I ran out of pears so I added an apple for a suprisingly pleasing taste.

-Katie Barkman

French Rhubarb Pie

1 pie crust, unbaked
1 egg, beaten
1 c. white sugar
2 c. rhubarb, diced

1 tsp. vanilla
1/4 tsp. salt
2 Tbsp. flour

TOPPING:
3/4 c. flour
1/2 c. brown sugar

1/3 c. margarine or
   butter, melted

Mix egg, white sugar, rhubarb, vanilla, salt and flour with a spoon. Pour rhubarb mixture into pie crust. Crumb flour, brown sugar and butter together; spread on top of rhubarb. Bake at 400° for 10 minutes. Reduce temperature to 350° and bake for 30 minutes longer or until done.

-Louise Marner

Rhubarb Crumb Pie

3 c. rhubarb, sliced
1 c. white sugar
1 Tbsp. cornstarch, heaping
2/3 c. cream

1 egg
1 Tbsp. butter
1 pie crust, unbaked

TOPPING:
1/3 c. butter
1/2 c. brown sugar

3/4 c. flour

Place rhubarb in pie crust. Mix white sugar, cornstarch, cream and egg together. Pour over rhubarb. Dot with 1 Tbsp. butter. Mix brown sugar and flour together. Cut in 1/3 c. butter until crumbly. Sprinkle over rhubarb mixture. Bake at 350° for 40 minutes or until golden brown.

-Carol Miller

Apple Cream Pie

4 c. tart apples, peeled
  and thinly sliced
2 Tbsp. sugar
2 Tbsp. lemon juice
1/4 c. butter
8 oz. cream cheese,
  softened
9" pie crust, baked

1 1/2 c. milk, cold
1 small pkg. instant
  vanilla pudding
1 tsp. lemon rind,
  grated
1/4 c. apricot
  preserves, melted

Sauté apples, sugar and lemon juice in butter until apples are tender; cool. Beat cream cheese until smooth. Gradually beat in 1 c. milk, dry pudding mix and lemon rind. Add remaining milk; beat until thickened. Spread in crust and arrange apples over filling; brush with preserves. Refrigerate 1 hour.

-Ruth Weaver

Apple Crumb Pie

5-6 apples, peeled
  and sliced
1 c. white sugar

2 Tbsp. flour
1 tsp. salt
1 pie crust, unbaked

CRUMB TOPPING:
1 c. flour
1/2 c. butter, firm

1/2 c. brown sugar

Mix white sugar, 2 Tbsp. flour and salt together. Add apples and stir to coat. Place in pie crust. Combine 1 c. flour and brown sugar. Cut in butter until crumbly. Place on top of apples. Bake at 425° for 15 minutes, then reduce temperature to 350° and bake for 1 hour longer.

-Edna Weaver

Chocolate Silk Pie

9" pie crust, baked
3/4 c. butter
1 c. sugar
2 oz. unsweetened
  chocolate, melted & cooled

1 tsp. vanilla
3 eggs

TOPPING:
1 c. heavy cream
2 Tbsp. confectioners' sugar

1/2 tsp. vanilla
chocolate, grated

Cream the butter and sugar until light and fluffy. Add choco-late and vanilla; beat until sugar is dissolved. Add eggs, 1 at a time, beating on high for 2 minutes after each addition. Spoon into cooled pie crust. In a separate bowl, beat cream and confectioners' sugar until stiff peaks form. Fold in vanilla. Cover top of pie with whipped cream; garnish with grated chocolate. Serves 8 people.

-Julie Hershberger

"Peace is not the absence of conflict,
but the presence of God
no matter what the conflict."
-Anonymous

Pumpkin Pie

1 3/4 c. pumpkin, cooked &
  mashed or canned
1/2 tsp. salt
1 3/4 c. milk
3 eggs, separated
2/3 c. brown sugar,
  firmly packed

2 Tbsp. granulated
  sugar
1 1/4 tsp. cinnamon
1/2 tsp. ginger
1/2 tsp. nutmeg
1/4 tsp. cloves
9" pie crust, unbaked

Bring milk to a boil and then set aside. In a bowl, mix pump-kin, salt, brown sugar, granulated sugar, cinnamon, ginger, nutmeg and cloves. Add egg yolks to pumpkin mixture. Beat egg whites in a separate bowl until stiff. Add egg whites to pumpkin mixture. Pour milk over top of pumpkin and stir slightly. Pour into pie crust. Bake at 450° for 15 minutes, then decrease temperature to 350° and bake for 15 minutes longer. Serves 6 people.

-Erma Hershberger

Crustless Pumpkin Pie

1/2 c. Bisquick
1 c. evaporated lowfat milk
3 egg whites
1 c. pumpkin
1/2 c. sugar

1 1/2 tsp. pumpkin
  pie spice
1 Tbsp. butter,
  softened
1 tsp. vanilla

Mix ingredients together until blended. Pour into a greased 9" pie pan. Bake at 350° for 35-40 minutes.

-Angie Peck

Pumpkin Custard Pie

9" pie crust, unbaked
1/2 c. pumpkin
1/4 c. brown sugar
1/4 c. white sugar
2 eggs, separated
1 Tbsp. flour
1/4 tsp. salt

1/4 tsp. cinnamon
1/4 tsp. pumpkin pie
spice
2 Tbsp. Karo syrup
2 Tbsp. butter, melted
1 1/4 c. milk

Combine pumpkin, brown sugar, white sugar and egg yolks. Set egg whites aside. Add flour, salt, cinnamon and pie spice. Mix in Karo, butter and milk. Whip egg whites until stiff. Add to pumpkin mixture. Pour into pie crust. Bake at 400° for 10 minutes; reduce temperature to 350° and bake for 30 minutes longer.

-Malinda Yoder

Pie Crust in a Pan

1 1/2 c. flour
2 Tbsp. milk
1/2 c. vegetable oil

1 tsp. salt
1 Tbsp. sugar

Place flour in a 9" pie pan. Make a hole in the flour. Place milk, vegetable oil, salt and sugar in the hole. Stir and press out with your fingers, to fit the pie pan.

-Ruth Weaver

Pie Crust

6 c. flour
2 c. shortening
1 egg

1 Tbsp. vinegar
  or lemon juice
1 c. milk

Place flour in a large bowl; cut in shortening until crumbly. Set aside. In a separate bowl, mix egg and vinegar; add milk. Slowly combine milk mixture with flour crumbs, cutting with a pastry cutter or using your hands. Mixture will be slightly wet. Let stand 5 minutes. Roll out onto a floured surface. Yield: 6 single pie crusts or 3 double crusts.

-Erma Hershberger

"Sweet" Pie Crust

1 1/2 c. flour
2 Tbsp. sugar
1 1/2 sticks unsalted
  butter, chilled

2 Tbsp. ice water

In a large bowl, whisk flour and sugar together. Cut butter into 12 pieces and distribute butter evenly over flour. Rub into flour with your fingertips. Sprinkle water over mixture while tossing with a fork. Knead dough for several turns on a lightly floured surface to bring together. Shape dough into a ball and refrigerate for at least 1 hour. Roll dough into a circle 2" larger than pie pan. Fit dough into a 9" pie pan. Keep refrigerated until ready to fill. NOTE: If prebaking crust, refrigerate for at least 30 minutes before baking.

-Beth Ernst

Basic Scones

2 c. flour
1 Tbsp. baking powder
2 Tbsp. sugar
1/2 tsp. salt

6 Tbsp. butter
1/2 c. buttermilk or
   milk
1 egg, lightly beaten

Mix flour, baking powder, sugar, and salt. Cut in butter. Mix well and add milk. Mix until dough is clingy and a bit sticky; do not overmix. Turn dough onto a floured surface and shape into round discs about 1 1/2" thick. Brush with egg. Bake on an ungreased baking sheet at 425° for 10-20 minutes or until lightly browned. Serve with "Moch Devonshire Cream" (see next recipe). NOTE: The secret to tender scones is little handling.

-Kathy Torrence

Moch Devonshire Cream

1/2 c. heavy cream or 8 oz.
   cream cheese, softened
2 Tbsp. powdered sugar

1/2 c. sour cream

In a chilled bowl, beat cream until stiff peaks form, adding sugar at the last minute. If you are using cream cheese, stir cream cheese and sugar together. Fold in sour cream until blended. Serve with "Basic Scones" (see above recipe).

-Kathy Torrence

Baklava

3 c. pecans, walnuts or
  almonds, finely chopped
2 tsp. cinnamon
1/2 tsp. nutmeg
1/4 tsp. cloves

1 1/2 c. margarine or
  butter, melted
16 oz. frozen fillo
  leaves, thawed

SYRUP:
1 1/2 c. sugar
1 1/2 c. water

2 Tbsp. lemon juice
3/4 c. honey

To prepare the syrup, heat sugar, water and lemon juice to boiling. Stir until sugar is dissolved. Boil 5 minutes. Remove from heat. Stir in honey and cool. In a separate bowl, combine nuts, cinnamon, nutmeg and cloves. Brush bottom and sides of a 15 1/2"x10 1/2" jellyroll pan with some margarine. Unfold fillo leaves. Cover with a damp towel to prevent drying. Carefully separate 1 leaf; place in a pan, folding edges over to fit pan, if necessary. Brush lightly with margarine. Repeat 6 times. Sprinkle 1 1/2 c. of the nut mixture evenly on the top. Layer 7 more fillo leaves in the pan, brushing each leaf with margarine. Sprinkle with remaining nut mixture. Layer remaining fillo leaves over nuts, brushing each leaf with margarine. With a sharp knife, cut pastry into 6 strips, 1 1/2" deep and 1 3/4" wide, lengthwise. Make diagonal cuts across the strips 1/2" deep and 2" wide. Pour remaining margarine over top. Bake at 350° until golden brown, approximately 1 hour-1 hour and 25 minutes. Place pan on a wire rack. Pour honey syrup over top and cool. Cut along scored lines. Serves 36 people.

-Rita Gerber

Lemon Curd

4 eggs
2 c. sugar
1 c. butter, melted
2/3 c. lemon juice

3 Tbsp. lemon peel,
  grated
1/8 tsp. salt

In the top of a double boiler, beat eggs and sugar. Stir in butter, lemon juice, peel and salt. Cook over simmering water for 15 minutes or until mixture is thickened and reaches 160°. Cover and store in the refrigerator for up to 1 week. Serve chilled with scones, biscuits or English muffins. Yield: 3 1/2 c.

-Erma Yoder

Very Cherry Crescent Bars

2 pkg. crescent rolls
16 oz. cream cheese, softened
1 c. sugar
10 oz. maraschino cherries,
  drained and chopped

3/4 c. walnuts,
  chopped
1 tsp. almond extract

Place 1 pkg. of crescent rolls in the bottom of a 9"x13" baking pan. Combine cream cheese, sugar, cherries, walnuts and almond extract. Spread over crescent rolls. Place the 2nd pkg. of crescent rolls on top. Bake at 375° for 30-35 minutes. Cool before cutting.

-Ann Miller

Pecan Tarts

CRUST:
2 c. flour
2 sticks butter

6 oz. cream cheese

FILLING:
5 eggs
2 c. light Karo syrup
1 c. brown sugar
1/2 tsp. salt

2 tsp. vanilla
2 Tbsp. butter
Pecans, crushed

To make the crust, combine butter with cream cheese and knead in flour. Refrigerate dough for 10 minutes. Press into large muffin tins. If using small muffin tins adjust baking time accordingly. To make filling, beat eggs. Add brown sugar, Karo, salt, vanilla and butter. Put a teaspoon (or more as desired) of crushed pecans in each tart and add filling on top. Bake at 400° for 10 minutes; reduce temperature to 350° and bake for 20 minutes longer. Yield: 24 tarts

-Naomi Gingerich

"Find out how much God has given you
and from it take what you need;
the remainder is needed by others."

-Saint Augustine

Cream Cheese Strudel

2 pkg. crescent rolls
16 oz. cream cheese
Cinnamon/sugar mixture

1 tsp. vanilla
2 Tbsp. butter, melted
1 c. sugar

GLAZE:
1 1/2 c. confectioners' sugar

2-3 Tbsp. milk

Place 1 pkg. of crescent rolls in the bottom of a 9"x13" pan. Mix cream cheese, sugar and vanilla. Spread cream cheese mixture on top of crescent rolls. Place the 2nd pkg. of crescent rolls on the top. Drizzle with butter. Sprinkle cinnamon/sugar on top. Bake at 350° for 30-35 minutes. NOTE: To make the Danish variation, spread a thin layer of fruit on top of cream cheese layer. Place the 2nd pkg. of crescent rolls on the top. Bake without cinnamon/sugar and butter at 350° for 30-35 minutes. Combine confectioners' sugar and milk to glaze consistency. Drizzle on top after Danish has finished baking. Serves 12-15 people.

-Wanda Schrock/Barbara Hershberger

"Contentment is worth
more than riches."

-German Proverb

Pecan Or Walnut Tarts

CRUST:

1 c. butter or margarine	2 1/2 c. flour, unsifted
6 oz. cream cheese	1/4 tsp. salt

FILLING:

1/2 c. pecans or walnuts, chopped	3/4 c. light Karo syrup
3 eggs, slightly beaten	3 Tbsp. butter, melted
1 1/2 c. brown sugar	1/8 tsp. salt
	3/4 tsp. vanilla

To make the crust, soften butter and cream cheese to room temperature. Mix salt and flour together. Add butter and cream cheese and flake with a fork. Divide dough into 2 parts, rolling into a cylinder about 1-2" in diameter. Chill dough. Slice dough then line mini muffin tins with the dough. Mix eggs, brown sugar, Karo, butter, salt and vanilla. Place a small amount of nuts in the bottom of the tart. Add filling and top with more nuts. Bake at 350° for approximately 20 minutes.

-Alma Spires/Kathy Marner

"Go often to the house of a friend,
for weeds choke an unused path."
-Ralph Waldo Emerson-

Cinnamon Twist Biscuits

1/3 c. shortening
1 3/4 c. flour
2 1/2 tsp. baking powder
3/4 tsp. salt
3/4 c. milk

1/2 c. margarine,
  melted
1 c. granulated sugar
2 tsp. cinnamon

Mix flour, salt and baking powder into a bowl. Cut in shortening, using a pastry blender or fork, until mixture is crumbly. Stir in just enough milk so that dough leaves the side of the bowl and forms a ball. Turn dough onto a lightly floured surface and knead 10 times. Roll out dough to 1/2" thick. Cut biscuits with a doughnut cutter. Dip biscuits into margarine. Mix cinnamon and sugar together. Dip buttered dough into the cinnamon/sugar mixture. Twist biscuits into a figure 8 and place on a baking sheet. Bake at 450° for 10-12 minutes.

-Carol Yoder/Katie Barkman

209

"Let us be grateful to people who
make us happy; they are the charming
gardeners who make our souls blossom."

-Marcel Proust-

Desserts

Baked Apples

Apples, peeled and halved
3/4 c. brown sugar
2 Tbsp. flour

Cinnamon (to taste)
Whipped cream
Water

Line the bottom of 2 pie pans or a 9"x13" pan with apples. Mix brown sugar, flour and cinnamon. Sprinkle over apples. Drizzle just enough water over apples and sugar mixture to moisten. Bake at 350° until apples are soft. Serve with whipped cream. Very quick & delicious!

-Geneva Schlabach

Baked Apples
Grandma Carr's Special Recipe

Apples
Walnuts, halved (optional)
1 tsp. vanilla

Butter
Cinnamon

SAUCE:
2 c. brown sugar
4 Tbsp. flour

2 c. milk
2 Tbsp. butter

Peel, cut and core apples. Place apples in ungreased baking pan. Dab with butter and sprinkle cinnamon on top. Bake at 350° until tender, approximately 1/2 hour. In a saucepan combine sauce ingredients and cook until thick. Stir in vanilla. Spoon over apples and put a walnut in center of the apple. Eat when cooled. NOTE: Sauce makes a very large batch.

-Dena Green

Delicious Apple Crispette

4 c. apples
1/2 c. brown sugar
1 tsp. cinnamon

2 tsp. clear jel
1/2 c. water

TOPPING:
1/2 c. water
3/4 c. white sugar
3/4 c. brown sugar

1 c. flour
5 Tbsp. butter

Peel and slice apples. Place in a shallow pan. Stir brown sugar, cinnamon, clear jel and water together. Cover apples with this mixture. To make topping, cut butter into sugars and flour. Stir in water and pour over apples. Do not stir together. Bake at 350° for 45 minutes. Cool and cut into squares. Serve with ice cream or whipped cream.

-Elsie Schrock

My Favorite Apple Crisp

1/2 c. white sugar
1/2 c. brown sugar
3/4 c. flour
1/4 c. butter

Apples, pared & sliced
1/4 c. water
Cinnamon

Work sugars, flour and butter together with fingers until crumbly. Grease a 9"x13" pan. Place enough apples in pan to fill it. Pour water over apples and generously sprinkle with cinnamon. Spread crumb mixture over apples and bake uncovered at 350° for 50 minutes. Serve warm with ice cream. NOTE: You can double the crumb mixture depending on how many people you are serving.

-Christina Troyer

School's Apple Crisp

7 large apples, peeled
  and sliced fine
3/4 c. white sugar

1 1/2 Tbsp. flour
1/4 tsp. salt
2 tsp. cinnamon

TOPPING:
3/4 c. quick oatmeal
3/4 c. brown sugar
3/4 c. flour
1/4 tsp. baking soda

1/4 tsp. baking powder
1/3 c. butter
1 tsp. cinnamon

Combine white sugar, 1 1/2 Tbsp. flour, salt and 2 tsp. cinnamon. Pour over apples. Mix well. Pour into greased, oblong cake pan. Mix dry ingredients for topping together. Cut in the butter until you have nice crumbs. Place crumbs on top of apples. Bake at 350° for 35-40 minutes. Serves 6-8 people.

-Charlene Miller

Caramel Apple Pizza

18 oz. sugar cookie dough
8 oz. cream cheese, softened
1/2 c. peanut butter
1/2 c. brown sugar, packed
4 c. tart apples,
  peeled and sliced

12 oz. lemon-lime soda
1 tsp. cinnamon
1/2 c. caramel ice
  cream topping
1/3 c. pecans, chopped
2 Tbsp. milk

Press cookie dough into a greased 14" pizza pan. Bake at 350° for 20 minutes or until golden brown. Run a large flat spatula under crust to loosen from pan. Cool on a wire rack. In a mixing bowl, beat cream cheese, peanut butter, brown sugar and milk until smooth. Spread over cooled crust. In a separate bowl, combine apples and soda. Drain well. Toss apples with cinnamon. Arrange over cream cheese mixture. Drizzle with caramel topping and sprinkle with pecans. Cut into wedges. Serves 8-10 people.

-Katie Barkman

Quick Apple Cobbler

2 cans apple pie filling
2 tubes buttermilk biscuits

1 tsp. cinnamon
Whipped topping

Place pie filling in 13"x9" pan. Sprinkle with cinnamon. Separate each biscuit into 3 layers and arrange over apples. Bake at 400° for 15-20 minutes until biscuits are brown. Garnish with whipped topping. Serves 8 people.

-Carol S. Miller

Apple Dumplings

3 apples, peeled and halved

SAUCE:
2 c. sugar
1/2 tsp. cinnamon

2 c. water
1/4 c. butter

CRUST:
2 c. flour
2 tsp. baking powder
3/4 c. shortening

Milk
1 tsp. salt

CENTER FILLING:
Dab of butter
1 tsp. brown sugar

Dash of cinnamon

Simmer sauce ingredients in a saucepan for 5 minutes and set aside. Mix crust ingredients together, using enough milk to moisten. Roll and cut dough into 5" squares. Place 1/2 an apple on each square. Fill center of the apple with Center Filling ingredients. Wrap dough over apple. Arrange dumplings in greased pan. Pour sauce over each dumpling. Bake at 375° for 35 minutes. Serves 6 people.

-Dean & Arvilla Kaufman

Cherry Pot Pie

1 qt. sour cherries, frozen   1 qt. water
1 c. brown sugar

DOUGH:
2 c. Bisquick   2/3 c. milk

In a large kettle, bring water, brown sugar and cherries to a boil. Combine Bisquick and milk together. Stir with fork until soft dough forms. Drop dough by the spoonful into boiling cherry mixture. Make sure the cherry mixture continues boiling while you are spooning in the dough. When all the dough is in the mixture, boil uncovered for 5 more minutes. Reduce heat, cover and cook for an additional 15 minutes. Remove from heat and allow to cool for 5 minutes before serving. Spoon into bowls and add milk, if desired. Serves 6-8 people. NOTE: This is a Stutzman Family recipe that has been passed down through several generations.

-Naomi Gingerich

Mrs. Morgan's Good Recipe

1 can Thank You lemon   12-13 oz. Cool Whip
  pie filling   Walnuts, chopped
1 can Eagle Brand milk   (optional)
1 large can crushed   Maraschino cherries
  pineapple, drained   (optional)
1 can mandarin oranges,
  drained

Combine pie filling, milk, pineapple and oranges together in large bowl and mix well. Place in a 13"x9" pan. Sprinkle with walnuts or maraschino cherries. Chill overnight.

-Lois Smith

Fresh Peach Cobbler

2 1/4 Tbsp. cornstarch
3/8 c. brown sugar
3/4 c. water
6 c. sweetened peaches, sliced

1 1/2 Tbsp. butter
1 1/2 Tbsp. lemon
  juice
1 Tbsp. white sugar

BATTER TOPPING:
1 1/2 c. flour, sifted
1 1/2 c. sugar
1 1/2 tsp. baking powder
3 eggs, slightly beaten

3/4 tsp. salt
6 Tbsp. butter,
  softened

Mix cornstarch, brown sugar and water. Add peaches and cook until mixture is thickened. Add butter and lemon juice. Pour into 13"x9" baking dish. Mix Batter Topping ingredients and put on top of peach mixture. Sprinkle white sugar on top. Bake at 400° for 40-50 minutes. Serve with milk or 2 c. heavy whipping cream, beaten until thick, mixed with 4 Tbsp. honey and 1 tsp. cinnamon.

-Alma Spires

Old-Fashioned Shortcake

2 c. flour
1 Tbsp. baking powder
1/3 c. sugar
3/4 tsp. salt

1/2 c. butter or
  margarine
1 egg, slightly beaten
1/2 c. milk

Mix flour, baking powder, sugar and salt thoroughly. Cut in butter. Make a small well in the center of flour mixture and pour egg and milk in center. Mix with fork until blended. Drop by heaping tablespoons on greased cookie sheet. Bake at 425° for 12-15 minutes. Serve shortcake hot, topped with strawberries and milk. Sweeten to taste. Serves 6 people.

Date Nut Pudding

1 c. dates, chopped
1 c. water, boiling
1 tsp. baking soda
1 c. sugar
2 Tbsp. butter, melted

1 egg
1 c. flour
1/2 c. nuts
Whipped cream
Bananas

Stir dates, water and baking soda together. Add sugar, butter, egg, flour and nuts. Pour ingredients into a cake pan. Bake at 350° until done to the touch. Cut into bite size pieces. Place in bowl, layering date cake, whipped cream and bananas until bowl is full.

-Erma Hershberger

Crazy Date Pudding

2 c. brown sugar
4 c. water, hot

1/2 c. butter

DOUGH:
2 c. flour, sifted
2 c. white sugar
4 tsp. baking powder
1/4 tsp. salt

2 c. dates, chopped
1 c. walnuts,
  chopped
1 c. milk

In a saucepan, mix brown sugar, water and butter. Boil for 2-3 minutes; set aside. In a mixing bowl, combine flour, white sugar, baking powder, salt, dates, walnuts and milk. Spread dough evenly in a 9"x13" baking dish and pour the brown sugar mixture on top. Bake at 350° for 45 minutes. Cool and cut into squares. Top with whipped cream.

-Elsie Schrock

Date Pudding

1 c. dates, chopped
1 c. water, boiling
1 Tbsp. butter
1 tsp. baking soda
Pinch of salt

1 c. sugar
1 1/2 c. flour
1/2 c. nuts, chopped
1 egg

CARAMEL SAUCE:
2 Tbsp. butter
1 c. brown sugar
2 c. water, boiling
2 Tbsp. cornstarch or clear jel

1/4 tsp. salt
Water
1 Tbsp. vanilla

To make caramel sauce, brown the butter. Add brown sugar and water; heat to boiling. In a separate bowl, stir together cornstarch, salt and enough water to make a smooth paste. Add to sugar mixture and stir until clear. Mix in vanilla. Cool.

To make date pudding combine dates, butter and soda in a bowl. Pour water over them. Let set until cooled. Add salt, sugar, flour, nuts and egg. Bake at 350° for 20-30 minutes. When cool, cut into pieces and serve in layers with whipped cream and caramel sauce. NOTE: This looks nice in a trifle dish.

-Esther Yoder

"Use what talents you have. The woods would have little music if only the best birds sang."
Reverend Oliver G. Wilson

Date Pudding

1 c. dates
1 tsp. baking soda
1 c. water, boiling
1 c. sugar
1 egg

SAUCE:
1 c. pancake syrup
1/2 c. sugar
1/2 c. water
1/2 c. milk
2 Tbsp. cornstarch

1 Tbsp. butter
1 c. flour
1/2 c. nuts
Bananas
Cool Whip

2 Tbsp. flour
1 1/2 tsp. vanilla
Butter (the size of
   an egg)

Place dates and baking soda in a bowl. Pour water over them and let stand to cool. In a separate bowl, mix sugar, egg, butter, flour and nuts. Combine with date mixture. Pour into a baking dish and bake at 350° for 30 minutes. Cool and cut in cubes. To make sauce, cook pancake syrup, sugar, water, milk, cornstarch and flour over low heat until it thickens. Add vanilla and butter. Stir and let cool. Serve pudding with sauce, bananas and Cool Whip.

-Steve & Lori Frink

Snicker Bar Dessert

4 large snicker bars,
   chopped
1/2 c. mayonnaise
1/2 c. walnuts or pecans

2 large red apples,
   diced but not peeled
8 oz. Cool Whip

Mix ingredients together and serve.

-Malinda Yoder

Baked Chocolate Fudge Pudding

3 Tbsp. butter
3/4 c. white sugar
1 c. flour
1/2 tsp. salt

1 1/2 tsp. baking
  powder
1/2 c. milk
1 1/4 c. water, boiling

TOPPING:
1 c. brown sugar
1/4 c. cocoa

1/4 t. salt

Cream butter and white sugar together. In a separate bowl, sift flour, salt and baking powder together. Add sifted mixture, alternating with milk, to the creamed mixture. Pour into an ungreased 9"x13" pan. To make topping, mix brown sugar, cocoa and salt. Sprinkle over top of batter. Do not stir. Pour boiling water over top of ingredients in pan. Bake at 350° for 40-45 minutes. Serve with ice cream.

-Ann Miller

Peanutty Chocolate Pudding

2 c. skim milk, cold
1 pkg. instant chocolate
  pudding

1/3 c. peanut butter
Whipped topping

In a mixing bowl, combine milk and pudding. Beat for 2 minutes. Add peanut butter and mix until smooth. Spoon into dessert dishes. Top with whipped topping. Ready in 15 minutes! Serves 4 people.

-Carol S. Miller

Glazed Pineapple Cheese Pie

15 1/4 oz. pineapple,
  crushed
Pineapple juice
16 oz. cream cheese,
  softened

1/2 c. sugar
2 eggs, beaten
1 tsp. vanilla
2 tsp. cornstarch
8" graham cracker crust

Drain pineapple, reserving juice. Blend cream cheese, sugar, eggs and 1/2 tsp. vanilla together. Stir in 1/2 c. pineapple. Pour over crust. Bake at 350° for 25-30 minutes or until center is set. Cool. Combine pineapple juice with cornstarch. Cook 3-4 minutes or until thickened and translucent. Stir in remaining vanilla, cool slightly. Pour over pie. Arrange remaining pineapple around outer edge of pie. Chill. Serves 6-8 people.

-Ruth Weaver

Chocolate Mocha Cheesecake

2 1/2 c. Oreos, crushed
1/2 c. butter, melted
8 oz. cream cheese
14 oz. Eagle Brand milk

2/3 c. Hershey's syrup
8 oz. Cool Whip
1 Tbsp. water, hot
2 Tbsp. instant coffee

Reserve some Oreos for the top of mixture. Mix remaining Oreos and butter together. Pat into a 9"x13" baking pan. Beat cream cheese until fluffy. Add Eagle Brand milk and Hershey's syrup together. In a separate bowl, mix water and instant coffee together; add to cream cheese mixture. Add Cool Whip and mix well. Pour over Oreo mixture. Top with Oreo halves and reserved crumbs. Drizzle with Hershey's syrup. Freeze. NOTE: Chill at least 4 hours.

-Ann Miller

Cheesecake

CRUST:
1 1/2 c. graham crackers, crushed

3 Tbsp. butter, melted

FILLING:
32 oz. cream cheese, softened

4 eggs

1 1/4 c. sugar

1 Tbsp. lemon juice

2 tsp. vanilla

TOPPING:
16 oz. sour cream

1/4 c. sugar

1 tsp. vanilla

Combine cracker crumbs and butter together. Press into bottom of a 10" springform pan. Set aside. To make filling, beat cream cheese in a mixing bowl until smooth. Add eggs, sugar, lemon juice and vanilla; mix thoroughly. Spoon over crust. Bake at 350° for approximately 50 minutes or until filling is almost set. Remove from oven and let stand 15 minutes, but leave oven on. Meanwhile, combine topping ingredients. Spread over cake and return to hot oven for 5 minutes. Cool to room temperature. Refrigerate 24 hours. Serve with your favorite fruit topping.

-Mary Ellen Troyer

Snow Cream

Clean snow

3 eggs, beaten

3 c. milk

1 1/2 c. sugar

3 tsp. flavoring, your choice

Combine eggs, milk, sugar and flavoring together; beat well. Add snow until it makes about a gallon. Serve and eat. Tastes mm'mm' good!

-Jesse and Jason Green

223

Cheesecake

1 large box lemon jello
8 oz. cream cheese
1 can evaporated milk, chilled
1 graham cracker crust

1 tsp. vanilla
1 small can pineapple, crushed and drained
1/2 c. sugar

Prepare jello as directed on the box. Add cream cheese and mix. Set aside. Beat milk until stiff and fluffy. Add sugar and vanilla. Add to jello mixture; it will be thin and light. Add pineapple. Pour into graham cracker crust (two 9" pie pans or one 9"x13" pan). Sprinkle a few graham cracker crumbs on top, if desired. Refrigerate until thick.

-Evangeline Pryor
(First Baptist Church, Dover, OH)

Caramel Fudge Cheesecake

1 pkg. fudge brownie mix
14 oz. caramels
1/4 c. evaporated milk
1 1/4 c. pecans, coarsely
  chopped
16 oz. cream cheese,
  softened

1/2 c. sugar
2 eggs
2 oz. semisweet
  chocolate squares,
  melted
2 oz. unsweetened
  chocolate squares,
  melted

Prepare brownie mix as directed on box. Spread into a greased 9" pan. Bake at 350° for 20 minutes. Cool 10 minutes. Melt caramels and milk together in microwave. Pour over brownie mixture. Sprinkle with pecans. Combine cream cheese and sugar; mix well. Add eggs, beating on low speed just until combined. Stir in chocolate. Pour over pecans. Bake at 350° for 35-40 minutes until center is almost set. Cool. Run knife around the edge of pan to loosen. Serves 12 people.

-Carol S. Miller

Cherry Gelatin Squares

12 oz. cherry gelatin
3 c. boiling water
2 1/2 c. lemon lime soda,
  chilled

2 cans cherry pie filling
Cool Whip or
  whipped cream
  (optional)

In a bowl, dissolve gelatin in water. Stir in pie filling. Mix well. Slowly add soda. Pour mixture into a 9"x13" dish. Cover and refrigerate until firm. Cut into squares. Put Cool Whip on top. Serves up to 12 people.

-Carol S. Miller

Pumpkin Cheesecake

1 1/2 c. graham cracker
  crumbs
5 Tbsp. butter, melted
1 c. + 1 Tbsp. sugar
24 oz. cream cheese,
  softened
1 tsp. vanilla

1 c. canned pumpkin
3 eggs
1/2 tsp. cinnamon
1/4 tsp. nutmeg
1/4 tsp. allspice
Whipped cream

To make the crust, combine graham cracker crumbs, butter and 1 Tbsp. sugar in a medium bowl. Stir well enough to coat all of the crumbs with the butter, but not too much; keep it crumbly. Press crumbs into the bottom and approximately 2/3 up the sides of a springform pan. Bake crust at 350° for 5 minutes. Set aside. In a large mixing bowl, combine cream cheese, 1 c. sugar and vanilla. Mix with an electric mixer until smooth. Add pumpkin, eggs, cinnamon, nutmeg, and allspice. Continue to beat until smooth and creamy. Pour filling into pan. Bake for 60-70 minutes. The top will be a bit darker at this point. Remove from oven and cool cheesecake to room temperature. Refrigerate. When cheesecake is chilled, remove from pan sides and cut into 8 pieces. Top with a generous portion of whipped cream. Serves 8 people.

-Marlin Yoder

"Fear less, hope more; eat less, chew more;
whine less, breathe more; talk less, say more;
love more, and all good things will be yours."

-Swedish proverb

Marble Cheesecake

CRUST:

1 c. graham cracker crumbs
3 Tbsp. sugar

3 Tbsp. butter

FILLING:

24 oz. cream cheese,
softened
3/4 c. sugar
Vanilla

3 eggs
1 unsweetened
chocolate square,
melted

Preheat oven to 350°. To prepare the crust, mix crumbs, sugar and butter. Press into the bottom of a 9" springform pan. Bake for 10 minutes. Increase oven temperature to 425°. Beat cream cheese, sugar and vanilla at medium speed with mixer until well blended. Add eggs, 1 at a time. Mix well. Blend chocolate with 1 c. of batter. Spoon plain and chocolate batter alternately over crust. Cut through batter with knife. Bake for 10 minutes. Reduce temperature to 250° and bake for 30 minutes. Loosen cake from rim of pan. Cool before removing rim of pan. Refrigerate.

-Erma Yoder

Pumpkin Delight

2 c. pumpkin
3 eggs, beaten
13 oz. evaporated milk
1 c. white sugar
1 c. brown sugar

3/4 tsp. salt
3/4 tsp. nutmeg
1 box white cake mix
1/2 c. butter, melted
1/3 c. nuts (optional)

In a large bowl, mix pumpkin, eggs, milk, sugars, salt and nutmeg. Pour into a large buttered 8"x12" pan. Sprinkle cake mix over top. Press into mixture. Drizzle butter over top. Sprinkle with nuts. Bake at 350° for 45-60 minutes. Serve warm with ice cream or whipped cream. Serves 15-18 people.

-Andrea Hostetler

Cheesecake
(For the Microwave)

CRUST:
1/4 c. butter
2/3 c. graham cracker
  crumbs
2 Tbsp. flour
1/3 c. + 5 Tbsp. sugar
1/4 tsp. cinnamon

8 oz. cream cheese
1 egg
1 tsp. lemon juice
1 c. sour cream
1/2 tsp. almond or
  vanilla flavoring

TOPPING:
1 can of fruit or garnish
  with fresh fruit: strawberries,
  blueberries, kiwi etc. (optional)

To make crust, melt butter in 9"x9" glass pan. Stir in graham cracker crumbs, flour, 2 Tbsp. sugar and cinnamon. Press into pan and set aside. Microwave the cream cheese for 30 seconds to soften. Add egg, 1/3 c. sugar and lemon juice to cream cheese. Beat until smooth. Pour on top of crust. Microwave on high for 5 minutes. Turn 1 time, halfway. In a separate bowl mix sour cream, 3 Tbsp. sugar and flavoring. Pour on top of baked mixture. Microwave on high for 2 minutes. Cool. Top with fruit.

-Lynette Miller

Pumpkin Roll

3 eggs
1 c. sugar
2/3 c. pumpkin, unspiced
1 tsp. lemon juice
3/4 c. flour
1 tsp. baking powder

2 tsp. cinnamon
1 tsp. ginger
1/2 tsp. salt
1/2 tsp. nutmeg
nuts, chopped
 (optional)

FILLING:
1 c. powdered sugar
4 Tbsp. butter

8 oz. cream cheese
1/2 tsp. vanilla

Beat eggs at high speed for 5 minutes. Gradually add sugar. Stir in pumpkin and lemon juice. Set aside. In a separate bowl, stir flour, baking powder, cinnamon, ginger, salt and nutmeg together. Fold in pumpkin mixture. Line jellyroll pan or 1" deep cookie sheet, with wax paper (or grease and flour it). Spread mixture in this pan and sprinkle with nuts. Bake at 375° for 15 minutes. Turn out onto towel sprinkled with powdered sugar. Roll up and let cool. To make filling beat powdered sugar, butter, cream cheese and vanilla until smooth. Unroll cake. Spread the filling on cake and roll back up. Chill.

-Marea Andreas

"Great things are not done by impulse,
but by a series of small things brought together."

-Vincent van Gogh

Pumpkin Ice Cream

CRUST:
2 c. graham cracker crumbs
1/4 c. butter, melted
1 Tbsp. powdered sugar
1/2 tsp. gelatin

FILLING:
1 1/2 qt. vanilla ice cream
3/4 c. pumpkin
1/2 c. sugar
1/2 tsp. salt
1/2 tsp. cinnamon
1/4 tsp. ginger
1/4 tsp. nutmeg
12 oz. Cool Whip, thawed

To make crust, combine crust ingredients. Reserve 1/3 c. crust mixture and pat remaining mixture into a 9"x13" pan. To make filling, scoop ice cream onto crumbs as evenly as possible. Mix remaining ingredients and spread over ice cream. Sprinkle with reserved crumbs. Serves 15 people.

-Andrea Hostetler

Dirt Dessert

16 oz. Oreo cookies, crushed
2 small boxes vanilla pudding, instant
12 oz. Cool Whip
8 oz. cream cheese, softened
1 c. powdered sugar
3 c. milk
1 stick margarine
1 can cherries
1 pkg. walnuts

Mix cream cheese, margarine and powdered sugar together. In a separate bowl, mix pudding and milk. Stir Cool Whip, pudding mixture and cream cheese mixture together. Use 1/2 - 3/4 cookies and layer on bottom of 9"x13" pan. Pour cream cheese mixture over cookie crumbs. Top with a layer of crumbled cookies, cherries and nuts. Refrigerate to make firm.

-Larcie H. Vines
(Greenville, NC)

Pumpkin Torte

CRUST:

1 1/2 c. graham crackers, crushed

1/3 c. sugar

1/2 c. butter or margarine

FILLING:

2 eggs

3/4 c. sugar

8 oz. cream cheese, softened

16 oz. pumpkin

3 egg yolks

1/2 c. milk

1/2 c. sugar

1/2 tsp. salt

1 tsp. cinnamon

1 envelope unflavored gelatin

1/4 c. water, cold

8 oz. whipped topping, thawed

Combine crust ingredients together. Press into the bottom of a 9"x13" baking pan. In a mixing bowl combine eggs, 3/4 c. sugar and cream cheese. Beat until smooth. Spread over crust. Bake at 350° for 20-25 minutes or until top appears set. Cool. In a saucepan, combine pumpkin, egg yolks, milk, sugar, salt and cinnamon. Cook, stirring constantly, until mixture thickens. Remove from heat. Dissolve gelatin in water. Add to saucepan. Fold in whipped topping. Spread over cooled torte. Chill. Serve with a dollop of whipped topping. NOTE: Torte keeps well for several days in the refrigerator. Serves 12-15 people.

-Barbara Hershberger/Wanda Schrock

Pumpkin Pie Dessert

CRUST:
1 box spice or yellow
  cake mix

1/2 c. butter, melted
1 egg

FILLING:
1/2 c. brown sugar,
  firmly packed
2/3 c. milk
15 oz. solid pumpkin

2 eggs
2 tsp. pumpkin pie
  spice

TOPPING:
1 c. cake mix
1/4 c. brown sugar,
  firmly packed

1/4 c. butter, softened
1/2 c. pecans,
  chopped

Whipped cream

Heat oven to 350°. In a large bowl, combine cake mix (reserve 1 c. for topping), butter and egg. Beat at low speed until well mixed, approximately 1-2 minutes. Spread in bottom of greased 9"x13" baking pan. Set aside. In same bowl, combine all filling ingredients. Beat at low speed until smooth. Pour over crust. In a medium bowl, combine topping ingredients, except pecans. Stir until crumbly. Stir in pecans. Sprinkle topping over filling. Bake for 45-50 minutes or until inserted knife comes out clean. Cool for 15 minutes. Serve warm or cool with whipped cream. Cover and store in refrigerator. Serves 15 people.

-Angie Gerber

Pumpkin
Streusel Custard

2 eggs
1/2 c. brown sugar, packed
1 tsp. vanilla
1/2 tsp. salt
1/2 tsp. cinnamon

1 c. evaporated milk
1/4 tsp. allspice
1/4 tsp. ginger
1/4 tsp. nutmeg
1 1/3 c. pumpkin, cooked or canned

TOPPING:
1 Tbsp. brown sugar
4 tsp. flour
2 tsp. butter or margarine, cold

4 Tbsp. pecans or walnuts, chopped
1/2 tsp. cinnamon

Beat eggs together. Add 1/2 c. brown sugar, vanilla, salt, 1/2 tsp. cinnamon, allspice, ginger and nutmeg. Stir in pumpkin and milk. Pour into greased baking pan. Bake at 325° for 20 minutes. To make topping, combine 1 Tbsp. brown sugar, flour and 1/2 tsp. cinnamon in small bowl. Cut in butter until crumbly. Stir in nuts. Sprinkle over custard and bake 15 minutes longer or until an inserted knife comes out clean. Serves 4 people.

-Fern Begly

Sweet Potato Crisp

16 oz. sweet potatoes,
  cooked and solid pack
1 can evaporated milk
1 1/2 c. sugar
1/2 or 1 tsp. nutmeg

3 eggs
1 box yellow cake mix
1 c. nuts, chopped
1 1/4 sticks butter,
  melted

ICING:
8 oz. cream cheese, softened
3/4 c. Cool Whip

2 c. powdered sugar

Mix sweet potatoes, milk, sugar, eggs and nutmeg. Pour mixture into a lightly greased 9"x13" baking pan that has been lined with wax paper. Sprinkle dry cake mix over sweet potato mixture. Sprinkle nuts over cake mix. Pat into cake mix. Pour melted butter over nuts. Bake at 325° for 50-60 minutes. Cool. Flip out onto serving dish. Peel off wax paper. To make icing, beat cream cheese, Cool Whip and powdered sugar together. Ice entire crisp. Refrigerate for 2-3 hours. Serves 10 people.

-Catherine Kelker
(First Baptist Church, Dover, OH)

"Great works are performed not by strength, but by perseverance."

-Samuel Johnson

Cranberry Brownie Torte

1 pkg. fudge brownie mix
2 eggs
1/2 c. oil

1/4 c. water
1/2 c. pecans,
   chopped

FILLING:
8 oz. cream cheese, softened
1/2 c. cranberry juice

2 Tbsp. sugar
Cool Whip

TOPPING:
1 can cranberry sauce
Pecans, halved (optional)

In a bowl, beat brownie mix, eggs, oil and water together. Fold in pecans. Transfer to a greased 10" round pan. Bake at 350° for 35-40 minutes or until toothpick comes out clean. Cool. Beat cream cheese, cranberry juice and sugar until smooth. Set aside 1 c. Cool Whip to garnish. Fold remaining Cool Whip into cream cheese mixture. Spread over cooled brownie. Stir cranberry sauce. Spread over filling. Garnish with Cool Whip and pecans. Refrigerate 2 hours before serving. Serves 12 people.

-Carol S. Miller

Banana Fluff

6 bananas
Sugar (to taste)
1 Tbsp. strawberry jam

1/2 pt. whipping
   cream
2 egg whites

Mash bananas. Add sugar and strawberry jam; whisk well. In a separate bowl, whip the cream. In another bowl, beat egg whites until stiff. Mix whipped cream and beaten egg whites together. Combine with banana mixture.

-Sharon Gerber
(John & Carol Berthelette Burkina Faso, Africa)

Tiramisu Toffee Dessert

10.75 oz. frozen pound cake,
  thawed and cut into 9 slices
3/4 c. coffee, strong
1 c. sugar
8 oz. cream cheese,
  softened

2 c. heavy whipping
  cream
2 Heath candy bars,
  chopped
1/2 c. chocolate
  syrup

Arrange cake slices on the bottom of 11"x7"x1.5" baking dish. Drizzle coffee over cake. Beat sugar, chocolate syrup and cream cheese in large bowl with electric mixer on medium speed until smooth. Add whipping cream. Beat on medium speed until light and fluffy. Spread over cake. Sprinkle with candy. Cover and refrigerate at least 1 hour, but no longer than 24 hours. Refrigeration is needed to set dessert and blend flavors. Serves 12 people.

-Vicki Yoder

Fat Free Cappuccino Flan

1 c. Egg Beaters
1/2 c. sugar
1 Tbsp. instant espresso
  or coffee powder
1/2 tsp. vanilla
1/8 tsp. cinnamon

2 1/3 c. skim milk,
  scalded & cooled for
  10 minutes
Light non-dairy
  whipped topping
Cocoa powder

Combine Egg Beaters, sugar, espresso, vanilla and cinnamon. Gradually stir in milk. Pour into 6 lightly greased 6 oz. custard cups. Set cups in a pan filled 1" in depth with hot water. Bake at 350° for 35-40 minutes or until an inserted knife comes out clean. Remove from pan. Cool to room temperature. Chill until firm, approximately 2 hours. To serve, loosen edges with knife and invert onto individual plates. Top with whipped topping and cocoa. Serves 6 people. NOTE: 120 calories per serving.

-Joanne Weaver

Cream Puff Dessert

1 c. water
1/2 c. butter

1 c. flour
4 eggs

FILLING:
8 oz. cream cheese,
  softened
2 small pkg. instant chocolate pudding

3 1/2 c. milk, cold

TOPPINGS:
8 oz. Cool Whip
1/4 c. chocolate
  ice cream topping
1/4 c. caramel
  ice cream topping

1/3 c. almonds,
  chopped

In a saucepan, bring water and butter to a boil over medium heat. Add flour, all at one time; stir until a smooth ball forms. Remove from heat. Let stand for 5 minutes. Add eggs, 1 at a time, beating well after each addition. Beat until smooth. Spread in a greased 9"x13" baking pan. Bake at 400° for 30-35 minutes until puffed and golden brown. Cool completely. To make filling, beat cream cheese, milk and pudding mix until smooth. Spread over puff. Refrigerate for 20 minutes. Spread Cool Whip over filling and refrigerate until ready to serve. Drizzle with chocolate and caramel toppings. Sprinkle with almonds.

-Christina Troyer/Carol S. Miller

"Do not be afraid of mistakes, providing you do not make the same one twice."

-Eleanor Roosevelt

Creamy Banana Pudding

14 oz. Eagle Brand milk,
  sweetened and condensed
1 1/2 c. water, cold
1 small pkg. instant
  vanilla pudding
2 c. Borden whipping cream, whipped

36 vanilla wafers
3 medium bananas,
  sliced and dipped
  in lemon juice from
  concentrate

In a large bowl, combine milk and water. Add pudding mix; beat well. Chill 5 minutes. Fold in whipped cream. Spoon 1 c. pudding mixture into a 2 1/2 qt. glass serving bowl. Layer with 1/3 of the wafers, 1/3 of the bananas and 1/3 of the pudding. Repeat layering two more times, ending with pudding. Chill. Garnish as desired. Refrigerate leftovers. NOTE: The vanilla wafers may be used whole or crushed.

-Sara Mae Stutzman

French Pudding

1/2 lb. vanilla wafers,
  crushed
1/4 lb. butter, softened
1 c. powdered sugar
2 eggs
1 pt. whipping cream

1/2 c. nuts, chopped
1/2 c. maraschino
  cherries, diced
Pinch of salt
1/2 tsp. vanilla

Grease a 2 qt. oblong baking dish. Line it with 1/2 of the vanilla wafers. Cream butter in a mixer, add powdered sugar gradually. Add eggs, 1 at a time, beating until fluffy after each addition. Spread mixture over wafers. Refrigerate. In a seperate bowl, beat the whipping cream. Add nuts, cherries, salt and vanilla. Spread over top of butter mixture. Top with remaining wafer crumbs. Keep refrigerated.

-Ellen Green

Asure (Noah's Pudding)
A Special Dessert From Turkey

1 c. wheat
1 c. raisins
1 c. apricots, dried and sliced
1 c. figs, dried
1 c. chickpeas

1 c. navy beans
3 c. sugar
4 bay leaves
10 cloves
16 c. water

GARNISH:
Nuts, shelled
Hazelnuts, peeled
Currants

Coconut
Pistachio
Pomegranate seeds

In separate bowls, soak chickpeas, navy beans and wheat in warm water for 24 hours. Boil wheat in 4 c. of the water that it was soaked in. After washing and straining the navy beans and the chickpeas, add them to the boiling wheat. When the chickpeas, navy beans and wheat are almost cooked, add bay leaves, cloves, apricots, figs and raisins. Boil at moderate heat for 20-25 minutes. Add sugar and boil 10 more minutes. The "Asure" will gradually get more dense. Once it gets dense, pour the "Asure" into serving cups. Garnish with nuts, hazelnuts, currants, pistachios, coconut and pomegranate seeds. Serve cold. NOTE: The name of this dessert is pronounced "ashureh". A delicious pudding that is made once each year in Turkey during the largest religious holiday. It is usually made in large quantities to share with neighbors.
*After the "Big Flood", Noah prepared the first meal for those who survived, with various kinds of legumes, sugar, dried fruit and spices on the ship.

-Lewis Kaufman
(Recipe by Chef Feridun Ugumu)

"Love is patient. Love is kind."

1 Corinthians 13:4

Canning
and
Freezing

Grape
Jelly

7-Day Sweet Pickles

7 lb. medium cucumbers
1 qt. vinegar
2 Tbsp. salt
7 c. white sugar

2 Tbsp. mixed pickle
  spice
Water, boiling

Cover cucumbers with boiling water and let stand for 24 hours. Repeat this process for 4 days, using fresh boiling water each time. On the 5th day, cut the cucumbers into 1/4" rings. In a saucepan, combine vinegar, salt, sugar and spice. Bring this to a boil, then pour over sliced pickles. Let stand 24 hours. On the 6th day drain vinegar to a saucepan and bring to a boil. Pour over pickles again and let set for 24 hours. On the 7th day drain off vinegar and bring to a boil. Add pickles and bring to the boiling point. Place in jars and seal. To seal: place hot pickles in hot jars with hot lids; pressure can at 5 lb. of pressure for 5 minutes; or water bath process for 15 minutes.

-Erma Hershberger

Bread & Butter Pickles

1 gallon cucumbers, sliced
4 small onions, sliced
1/2 c. salt
5 c. sugar
1 1/2 tsp. turmeric

2 tsp. mustard seed
1 tsp. celery seed
3/4 c. vinegar
4 c. water

Combine cucumbers, onions and salt. Set aside for 3 hours. Drain well and rinse. In a big kettle, mix sugar, turmeric, mustard seed, celery seed, vinegar and water together. Add cucumbers and onions. Bring to a boil. Place in warm jars, leaving a 1/2" headspace. Seal right away with hot lids and hot rings or water bath process for 10 minutes. Yield: 7 pints

-Erma Yoder

Canned Relish

3 large green peppers
12 cucumbers
6 large onions
1/3 c. salt
4 tsp. pickle spice
1 tsp. celery seed

1 tsp. turmeric
1 tsp. mustard powder
1 tsp. ginger
2 c. vinegar
3 c. sugar

Grind peppers, cucumbers and onions together. Add salt and stir. Let set for 1 hour. Drain. Put pickle spice, celery seed, turmeric, mustard powder and ginger in a spice bag. Add spice bag, vinegar and sugar to the vegetables and bring to a boil. Place in jars, leaving 1/2" headspace. Seal with hot lids and hot rings or water bath process for 10 minutes.
Yield: 6 pints

-Alma Spires

Relish

12 green tomatoes
6 small onions
1 1/4 oz. whole mixed
   pickle spice
4 c. brown sugar

6 red peppers
6 green peppers
1 small bunch of celery
2 c. vinegar
salt (to taste)

Grind tomatoes, onions, celery and peppers together. Place in a kettle, add vinegar, salt, pickle spice and brown sugar. Boil until it reaches desired thickness. Place in jars, leaving 1/2" headspace. Seal with hot lids and hot rings or water bath process for 10 minutes.

-Erma Hershberger

243

Relish

24 medium green tomatoes
6 green sweet peppers
6 hot peppers
8 medium yellow onions
2 red sweet peppers

6 Tbsp. canning salt
Celery seed
Mixed pickle spice
4 c. apple vinegar
2 c. sugar
Water, boiling

Grind tomatoes, peppers and onions in a food processor. Place them in a large saucepan and sprinkle with salt. Pour boiling water over them and let stand for 5 minutes. Drain water. In a large kettle, combine vinegar, sugar, spice and celery seed. Bring to a boil. Add vegetables and cook for 15 minutes. Pour into warm pint jars leaving 1/2" headspace. Seal with hot lids and hot rings or water bath process for 10 minutes.

-Kathryn Denmon
(First Baptist Church, Dover, OH)

Zucchini Relish

10 c. zucchini, ground
4 c. onion, ground
5 Tbsp. salt
2 1/4 c. vinegar
6 c. sugar
1 Tbsp. dry mustard
2 tsp. celery seed

1/4 tsp. black pepper
1 Tbsp. turmeric
1 Tbsp. nutmeg
1 tsp. cloves, ground
green food coloring
2-3 Tbsp. Clear Jel,
    pectin or perma flo

Combine zucchini, onions and salt. Let stand overnight. Drain and rinse 2 times. Add remaining ingredients and cook slowly for 30 minutes. Thicken with Clear Jel. Pour into jars, leaving 1/2" headspace and seal. Water bath process for 10-20 minutes.

-Carol Yoder

Canned Sauerkraut

Cabbage
1 tsp. salt

2 tsp. vinegar
Water, boiling

Shred cabbage and pack in quart jars. Make a hole in the center by inserting the handle of a wooden spoon. Add the salt, vinegar and water into the hole, leaving 1/2" headspace. Secure lids and let stand for 6 weeks. If the lids have not sealed after 6 weeks, water bath process for 10 minutes. It will be ready to eat in 6 weeks. Yield: 1 qt. jar.

-Alma Spires

Dilled Green Beans

3 lb. fresh green or
  yellow string beans
2 1/2 c. white vinegar
2 1/2 c. water
2 Tbsp. pickling salt
5 carrots, sliced

5-10 heads fresh dill
  or 2 1/2-5 tsp.
  dried dill seed
5-10 garlic cloves
1 small onion, sliced

Wash beans and trim ends. Cut into 4" lengths. In a 3 qt. saucepan, combine vinegar, water and pickling salt. Bring to a boil over high heat. Meanwhile, place 1-2 dill heads or 1/2-1 tsp. dried dill seed, 1-2 garlic cloves, 1 onion slice and 1 carrot slice in each hot pint jar. Firmly pack beans upright in jars, leaving a 1/2" headspace. Immediately pour the hot vinegar mixture over beans, leaving a 1/2" headspace. Carefully run a nonmetallic utensil down inside of jars to remove trapped air bubbles. Wipe tops and threads of jars clean. Place hot lids on jars and screw bands on firmly. Water bath process for 10 minutes. Yield: 5 pints

-Alma Spires

Canned Fruit

Fresh peaches, pears or cherries

SYRUP:

1 part hot water   1 part sugar

Combine water and sugar; bring to a boil. Put lids into boiling water for a few minutes. Fill jars with fruit and pour hot syrup over top, leaving 1/2" headspace. Wipe tops and threads of jars clean. Place hot lids on jars and screw rings on tightly. Pressure can at 5 lb. for 8 minutes or water bath process for 15 minutes.

-Erma Hershberger

Sloppy Joe Sauce

12 large tomatoes
4 medium onions
4 apples
1 red pepper
2 Tbsp. salt
1 tsp. cloves

1 tsp. cinnamon
1 tsp. allspice
1 c. water
2 c. vinegar
3 c. sugar
1 pkg. Sloppy Joe mix

Grind tomatoes, onions, apples and pepper. Add water, vinegar, salt, sugar and Sloppy Joe mix. Boil for 1 1/2 hours or until thick like ketchup. Add cloves, cinnamon and allspice approximately 5 minutes before removing from the stove. Pour into jars, leaving 1/8" headspace. Wipe tops and threads of jars clean. Place hot lids on jars and screw bands on firmly. Water bath process to seal for 15 minutes. To use, brown 2 lb. hamburger in a saucepan. Add 1 pt. of Sloppy Joe Sauce. Simmer until well blended and serve.

-Alma Spires

Chili Soup

4 lb. hamburger
4 medium onions
8 qt. tomato juice
64 oz. kidney beans
64 oz. pork-n-beans
4 Tbsp. chili powder
4 garlic cloves

Salt (to taste)
Pepper (to taste)
12 Tbsp. flour
1 1/3 c. water
1 c. brown sugar
1 c. ketchup

Brown hamburger and onions. Add tomato juice, beans, chili powder, cloves, brown sugar, ketchup, salt and pepper. In a bowl, combine flour and water to make a paste; add to soup. Bring to a boil, stirring constantly. Pour into jars, leaving 1" headspace, and secure with lids and rings. Water bath process for 3 hours or pressure can at 10 lb. for 70 minutes. Yield: 14 quarts

-Erma Yoder

Canned Apple Pie Filling

4 c. sugar
1 c. cornstarch or Clear Jel
3 tsp. cinnamon
1 tsp. nutmeg

1 tsp. salt
8-10 c. water
3 Tbsp. lemon juice
Apples, peeled & sliced

In a large kettle combine sugar, cornstarch, cinnamon, nutmeg and salt. Add water and cook until thickened, stirring constantly. Add lemon juice. Fill jars 1/3 full of sauce. Add apple slices, pushing them down into the sauce until the jar is filled. Put lids on and water bath process for 20 minutes. NOTE: Dot with butter when you make a pie or put on crumb topping.

-Alma Spires

Apple Dumplings (Freeze)

1 peck Yellow Delicious apples,
  halved, peeled and cored
6 c. flour
1 Tbsp. salt
2 1/4 c. Crisco
1 c. milk, warm

1 Tbsp. vinegar
1 tsp. white sugar,
  per apple
pinch of cinnamon,
  per apple

SAUCE:
2 c. brown sugar
2 c. water

1/4 c. butter
1/4 tsp. cinnamon

In a large bowl, mix flour, salt and Crisco until fine crumbs form. Add milk and vinegar. Work this as you would a pie crust. Roll out dough on a lightly floured surface. Cut into 6" squares. Place the bottom half of the apple on a square of dough. Fill the center of the apple with sugar and cinnamon. Place other half of apple on top and wrap with dough. Place 6 apple dumplings (or whatever combination you want) in a freezer bag and freeze. To scrve: Place 6-8 apple dumplings in a 9"x13" baking pan. Mix sauce ingredients and bring to a boil. Pour over apple dumplings. Bake at 350° for 1 hour. Serves 24 people.

-Erma Yoder

Grape Juice (Canned)

1 1/2 c. grapes, not pitted
1/2 c. white sugar

water

Place grapes in qt. jars. Add sugar then enough water to fill the jar. Secure with lids. Water bath process for 10 minutes. Leave set a few weeks before using. When ready to use, drain juice off the grapes and enjoy. Yield: 1 qt. jar.

-Alma Spires

V-8 Juice

1 peck tomatoes (with acid)
4 stalks celery
1 tsp. pepper
2-3 carrots
2 Tbsp. salt

1 green pepper
1 c. sugar
2 onions
4-5 Tbsp. vinegar

Cook all ingredients together until soft. Put through a Victorio Strainer or sieve. Pour hot liquid into jars, leaving 1/2" headspace. Secure with lids and bands. Water bath process for 20-30 minutes or pressure can at 10 lb. for 15 minutes.

-Kathy Marner

Corn to Freeze

Sweet corn
1 tsp. salt

2 tsp. white sugar
1/2 c. water

Cut corn off cobs without blanching. Measure corn into kettle and add sugar, salt and water according to the amount of corn you have. Bring to a boil, stirring constantly so that it doesn't scorch. Boil for 3 minutes. Cool as soon as possible. Place in containers and freeze. No extra seasoning is needed when heating to serve. Yield: 1 qt. of corn

-Alma Spires

"Faith is spelled: R-I-S-K."

-Tim Troyer-

General Index

SALADS AND SALAD DRESSINGS

SOUPS AND VEGETABLES

MEATS, SAUCES, AND MAIN DISHES

253

CAKES, COOKIES, AND CANDY

Favorite Recipes

_____

_____

_____

_____

_____

_____

_____

_____

_____

_____

_____

_____

_____

_____

_____

_____

_____

_____

_____

_____

_____

_____

Favorite Recipes

_____
_____
_____
_____
_____
_____
_____
_____
_____
_____
_____
_____
_____
_____
_____
_____
_____
_____
_____
_____
_____
_____
_____

Please Consider Purchasing
A Well-Watered Garden
For Your Friends and Loved Ones

A Well-Watered Garden • BCF Cookbook
PO Box 396 • Berlin, Ohio 44610

Please send me ____ copies of *A Well-Watered Garden* at $9.99
per book. I am enclosing $2.00 shipping and handling per
book ($1.00 for each additional book ordered).

Name _____

Address _____

City_____ State _____ Zip _____

A Well-Watered Garden • BCF Cookbook
PO Box 396 • Berlin, Ohio 44610

Please send me ____ copies of *A Well-Watered Garden* at $9.99
per book. I am enclosing $2.00 shipping and handling per
book ($1.00 for each additional book ordered).

Name _____

Address _____

City_____ State _____ Zip _____

Please Consider Purchasing
A Well-Watered Garden
For Your Friends and Loved Ones

A Well-Watered Garden • BCF Cookbook
PO Box 396 • Berlin, Ohio 44610

Please send me ___ copies of *A Well-Watered Garden* at $9.99 per book. I am enclosing $2.00 shipping and handling per book ($1.00 for each additional book ordered).

Name _____

Address _____

City_____ State _____ Zip_____

A Well-Watered Garden • BCF Cookbook
PO Box 396 • Berlin, Ohio 44610

Please send me ___ copies of *A Well-Watered Garden* at $9.99 per book. I am enclosing $2.00 shipping and handling per book ($1.00 for each additional book ordered).

Name _____

Address _____

City_____ State _____ Zip_____